Ch

Ethics

If the life of Jesus is not our pattern, the death of Jesus will not be our pardon.

Dr. John Hobbs

Heritage Publications
1106 Destiny Court
Wylie, Texas 75098

ISBN: 9781726891233

Table of Contents

Introduction

Ethics is defined as "the study of standards of conduct and moral judgment; moral philosophy; the system or code of morals of a particular person, religion, group, or profession; how one conforms to the standards of conduct of a given profession or group." Christian Ethics defines virtuous behavior and wrong behavior from a Christian perspective. The apostle Peter said that Christians **"should follow his (i.e. Christ's) steps"** (1 Pet. 2:21). Peter went on to say that Christians "might live unto righteousness" (1 Pet. 2:24). John wrote, **"He that saith he abideth in him ought himself also to walk even as he walked"** (1 John 2:6).

Paul wrote, "I therefore, the prisoner in the Lord, beseech you to walk worthily of the calling wherewith ye were called" (Eph. 4:1). He also said, "Only let your manner of life be worthy of the gospel of Christ" (Phil. 1:27). Again he stated, "To the end that ye should walk worthily of God, who calleth you into his own kingdom and glory" (1 Thess. 2:12). Again Paul stated that we are "to walk worthily of the Lord unto all pleasing, bearing fruit in every good work" (Col. 1:10).

The life of a Christian is to live as Jesus lived. His lifestyle should be our pattern. In 2 Corinthians 5:14-15 Paul wrote, **"For the love of Christ constraineth us; because we thus judge, that one died for all, therefore all died; and he died for all, that they that live should no longer live unto themselves, but unto him who for their sakes died and rose again."** Notice carefully that Christians are not to live unto themselves (i.e. be selfish and self-centered), but we are to "live unto him." **Very simply: if the life of Jesus is not our pattern, the death of Jesus will not be our pardon!**

Christian Ethics is based on two fundamental commandments. Jesus said that the first commandment is to **"love the Lord thy God with all thy heart, and with all thy soul, and with all thy mind, and with all thy strength"** (Mark 12:30). Notice the all-ness of the each part of the command. The second commandment is: **"Thou shalt love thy neighbor as thyself"** (Mark 12:31). In Matthew 22:40 Jesus said, "On these two commandments the whole law hangeth, and the prophets." Every command of God has these two commands as their background.

A True Story

Several years ago, a man said, "I am just a bad seed." He and his sister were given up for adoption when he was about four, and his sister was two. Certainly, this must have been a traumatic experience for him. He and his sister were adopted by a Christian couple who did not have children. They desperately wanted children but were unable to have any. The chance to adopt two young children was an answer to prayer. The Christian couple had a strong spiritual commitment. They went to church every time the doors were open. They prayed constantly. They believed in the authority of God's word. They set the right example for their two adopted children. They loved them deeply. They sent them to church camps. Even though the two adopted children had loving, faithful, Christian parents, the boy decided to live an evil life. He engaged in sexual immorality and rebelled against the Christian influence that had been set before him. When he was married, he committed adultery on his wife. Several Christian friends and relatives, who loved him, tried their best to get him to see the truth and the right path to follow. However, he continued to live a sinful, disobedient, unfaithful, ungodly life. His response to these Christians was "The reason I am the way I am is simply I am just a bad seed." He wanted to blame his sinful life on the fact that he had a bad beginning that he was unable to overcome. Let us analyze that statement biblically.

In Ecclesiastes 7:29 we read, **"God made man upright; but they have sought out many inventions."** Notice that "God made man upright." In other words, God made man sinless and pure. Men "go astray" from God—they are not born astray (Psa. 58:3). Jesus said, "Suffer the little children, and forbid them not, to come unto me: for to such belongeth the kingdom of heaven" (Matt. 19:14). Jesus was teaching that little children are born in a safe eternal condition. Children are not born sinners. Ezekiel 18:20 states, **"The soul that sinneth, it shall die: the son shall not bear the iniquity of the father, neither shall the father bear the iniquity of the son; the righteousness of the righteous shall be upon him, and the wickedness of the wicked shall be upon him."** Sin is not transmitted through the genes. Sin is a choice (Joshua 24:15; Deut. 30:15-20). Paul said, "I was alive apart from the law once" (Rom. 7:9). When was he "alive apart from the law"? When he was a baby! When Paul was a baby, he was spiritually alive—not spiritually dead! Regardless of the circumstances in which we are born, the salient fact is that our actions are a choice.

Some people are born in tough situations and have risen above their environment to be godly and successful. Why? How? Righteousness is a choice. An individual must face the fact that he will be rewarded for making good choices and suffer hardship for making wrong choices. A bad birth environment does not, cannot, and never will justify sinful practices! To claim "I am just a bad seed" is accusing God of doing something wrong which is absurd (Job 40:8). The Bible teaches we will be judged by what we have done in the body—not out of the body (2 Cor. 5:10; Eccl. 12:13-14). The apostle Paul wrote, **"So then each one of us shall give account of himself to God"** (Rom. 14:12). We cannot blame God or someone else for our sins. Adam tried to blame God for his sins when he said, "The woman whom thou gavest to be with me, she gave me of the tree. And I did eat" (Gen. 3:12). Adam's accusation was wrong then, and so is everyone else who blames God for their sinful practices. No one is born a bad seed. We are only bad when we choose to do bad! John said, **"He that doeth righteousness is righteous"** (1 John 3:7). We are only righteous when we choose to do righteousness.

Chapter 1-Authority in Morality

Christians today are confronted with many conflicting views of morality. People have different opinions concerning what is right and wrong. What once was generally accepted as good and true is now challenged. Governments are redefining the concept of marriage. Businesses often operate with ethics that sanction lying, deception, and stealing. How does one know what is right and wrong in the areas of morality? Everyone has been given a basic sense of right and wrong (Rom. 1:19), but the standard of right and wrong often differs from person to person. It is imperative that we examine very carefully the standard by which all questions of ethics and morality must yield.

What is "Not" our Authority in Ethics and Morality?

#1—Feelings

Many people say, "If it feels good, it must be right." Debby Boone sang, "It can't be wrong when it feels so right." Obi-Wan Kenobi said to Luke Skywalker, "Trust your feelings." People are following their feelings today en mass. We have Christians divorcing their mates because they do not "feel love." So, with no respect or regard to the word of God, they divorce and marry someone else. But, feelings are not the guide to Christian conduct! Feelings are based on what we believe, and what we believe is based on what we have been taught or heard or read. Jacob was told that his son Joseph was dead. He was even shown Joseph's coat with blood on it. Jacob believed what he was told and shown, and he grieved over the death of Joseph. But, the truth was that Joseph was not dead! Feelings do not determine truth. Proverbs 14:12 states, **"There is a way which seemeth right unto a man; But the end thereof are the ways of death."** Just because something feels right or seems right, that does not make it right.

#2--One's Own Conscience

The Blue Fairy told Pinocchio, "Always let your conscience be your guide." But, one's conscience is not always reliable. Our conscience tells us if we are doing right or wrong according to what our conscience believes. Our conscience is a creature of education, and we can "mis-educate" our conscience. In times past, Hindu women have taken their little infant babies and thrown them into the river to drown. They have walked away believing they had done right. Why? Because their Hindu priests told them to do it. Mark this point down— our conscience does not determine truth! Examine the life of Paul. In Acts 23:1 Paul said, "I have lived before God in all good conscience until this day." Paul "persecuted the church of God, and made havoc of it" (Gal. 1:13). This he did "beyond measure." In Acts 26:9 Paul said, **"I verily thought with myself** that I ought to do many things contrary to the name of Jesus of Nazareth." But, his thinking did not constitute truth! When Naaman was told how he could have his leprosy removed, he did not like the remedy. 2 Kings 5:11 states, "But Naaman was wroth, and went away and said,

Behold I thought, He will surely come out to me, and stand, and call on the name of Jehovah his God, and wave his hand over the place, and recover the leper." Naaman's thinking did not determine the truth. The basis of all ethics and morality is either in man or outside of man. The answer is that it is outside of man. Listen very carefully to these verses:

Prov. 3:5, **"Trust in Jehovah with all thy heart, and lean not upon thine own understanding."**

Prov. 3:7, **"Be not wise in thine own eyes."**

Prov. 23:4, **"Cease from thine own wisdom."**

Prov. 28:26, **"He that trusteth in his own heart is a fool."**

Isa. 5:21, **"Woe unto them that are wise in their own eyes, and prudent in their own sight."** The word "woe" means great sorrow, grief, and misery is coming upon you.

Jer. 10:23, **"O Jehovah, I know that the way of man is not in himself; it is not in man that walketh to direct his steps."**

Rom. 12:16, **"Be not wise in your own conceits."**

#3—The Majority

Some say, "Everyone is doing it." But, does the fact that the majority believes something or does something make it right? If you followed the majority in Noah's day, you would have perished in the flood. If you followed the majority in Joshua's day, you would have perished in the wilderness. Years ago the majority believed the earth was the center of the universe. Years ago the majority believed the earth was flat. Several years ago I was grading papers at a math contest. There were about 40 graders in the room. The majority believed that there was a wrong answer on the answer key. I was one of the majority. However, there was one teacher who was adamant that the answer key was correct. Since we had such respect for this teacher, we decided to accept his position. At the time, I did not agree with him. I thought he was wrong. When I went home and studied the problem, I discovered he was correct! The majority had been wrong. Exodus 23:2 states, "Thou shalt not follow a multitude to do evil." We would all do well to remember what Jesus said. In Matthew 7:13-14 Jesus said, **"Enter ye in by the narrow gate: for wide is the gate, and broad is the way, that leadeth to destruction, and many are they that enter in thereby. For narrow is the gate, and straitened the way, that leadeth unto life, and few are they that find it."** I quoted this one time to a school teacher and she said, "I disagree." She was not disagreeing with me. She was disagreeing with Jesus! He said this—not me! Jesus taught this same principle in Luke 13:22-30. Very simply—the majority does not determine truth.

#4—Another Person or One's Own Thinking

William Schulz, president of the Unitarian Universalist Association, said, "Each individual is the ultimate source of authority." Brethren, this is heresy of the highest order! No man has the right to make up the rules on what is right or wrong! Swami Muktananda wrote, "Kneel to your own self, honor and worship your own being. God dwells within you as you!" Philosopher L. L. Whyte says, "In dropping God, man recovers himself. It is time that God be put in his place, that is, in man, and no nonsense about it." Barbara Marx Hubbard, a New-Ager, wrote, "At this moment of our planetary birth each person is called upon to recognize that the 'Messiah' is within." Stuart Wilde taught that people are not to lean upon others metaphysically.

All of these men and women are teaching absolute heresy! According to these people, every person is his own god, and therefore does not need outside help. They teach that man is to look inside himself for all the answers of life. How foolish!

Oprah Winfrey had a grandmother who taught her that the Bible was the authority. But, Oprah said in essence, "I used to be troubled until I learned that the kingdom of God is within you. The answers to man's existence are within man and not from some external outside source." Oprah does not understand Luke 17:21. The verse means that "the kingdom" (i.e. the rule and reign of God) is an inward, spiritual concept. God rules and reigns in the hearts of those who submit to His will and follow His teachings. God's reign is spiritual. It is absolute and total heresy to teach that the answers to man's problems are within man (cf. Proverbs 3:5; 3:7; 23:4; 28:26; Isa. 5:21; 26:7; 55:8-9; Jer. 10:23; Matt. 4:4; Rom. 12:16; etc.).

Warnings To Be Heeded

Jesus warned us, "Beware of false prophets, who come to you in sheep's clothing, but inwardly are ravening wolves" (Matt. 7:15). He also said, "Every plant which my heavenly Father planted not, shall be rooted up. . . if the blind guide the blind, both shall fall into a pit" (Matt. 15:13-14). The apostle Paul warned us, **"And no marvel; for even Satan fashioneth himself into an angel of light. It is no great thing therefore if his ministers also fashion themselves as ministers of righteousness; whose end shall be according to their works"** (2 Cor. 11:14-15). Satan is our "adversary." If he appeared in a red suit with pointed horns, a pitch fork, and a red tail, we would very quickly be aware he was our enemy. But, Satan uses men and women who appear as ministers of light and righteousness. Therefore, we must be on our guard to recognize truth from error. The apostle Peter warns us, "But there arose false prophets also among the people, as among you also there shall be false teachers, who shall privily bring in destructive heresies, denying even the Master that bought them, bringing upon themselves swift destruction. And many shall follow their lascivious doings; by reason of whom the way of the truth shall be evil spoken of. And in covetousness shall they with feigned words make merchandise of you: whose sentence now from of old lingereth not, and their destruction slumbereth not" (2 Pet. 2:1-3). The apostle John also warned us, **"Beloved, believe not every spirit, but prove the spirits, whether they are of God; because many false prophets have gone out into the world"** (1 John 4:1).

We Have an Individual Responsibility to Study the Bible

Paul said, **"Wherefore be ye not foolish, but understand what the will of the Lord is"** (Eph. 5:17). In Acts 17:11 we read, "Now these were more noble then those in Thessalonica, in that they received the word with all readiness of mind, examining the scriptures daily, whether these things were so." Paul told Timothy, **"Give diligence to present thyself approved unto God, a workman that needeth not to be ashamed, handling aright the word of truth"** (2 Tim. 2:15). The words "give diligence" come from the Greek word *spoudazo* which means "work hard; do your best; give maximum effort." Are we as Christians working hard and giving maximum effort to understand the word of truth? If not, why not?

What Is Our Authority in Morals and Ethics?

Jesus said, "All authority hath been given unto me in heaven and on earth" (Matt. 28:18). Jesus delegated authority to His apostles. He told them, **"He that receiveth you receiveth me, and he that receiveth me receiveth him that sent me"** (Matt. 10:40). In John 13:20 Jesus said, "Verily, verily, I say unto you, He that receiveth whomsoever I send receiveth me; and he that receiveth me receiveth him that sent me." Therefore, to hear and listen and obey the apostles is to hear and obey Jesus! Jesus gave the apostles the authority and power to bind and loose in Matthew 16:19 and 18:18. Whatever the apostles taught is authoritative and binding. Before Jesus died and left for heaven, He told His apostles, "But the Comforter, even the Holy Spirit, whom the Father will send in my name, he shall teach you all things, and bring to your remembrance all that I said unto you" (John 14:26). In John 16:13 Jesus told His apostles, "Howbeit when he, the Spirit of truth, is come, he shall guide you into all the truth: for he shall not speak from himself; but what things soever he shall hear, these shall he speak: and he shall declare unto you the things that are to come."

In John 17:17 Jesus said, **"Sanctify them in the truth: thy word is truth."** Paul said, "And we know that the judgment of God is according to truth" (Rom. 2:2). Jesus also said, **"The scripture cannot be broken"** (John 10:35). In 2 Timothy 3:16-17 Paul wrote, **"Every scripture is inspired of God is also profitable for teaching, for reproof, for correction, for instruction which is in righteousness: that the man of God may be complete, furnished completely unto every good work."** Here is the answer to the question: "What Is Our Authority in Morals and Ethics?" Scripture is the authority! It is not what you say or I say or what someone else says—it is Scripture! Scripture provides us with everything we need—for teaching, reproof, correction, and instruction in right-doing! Jesus said, **"Man shall not live by bread alone, but by every word that proceedeth out of the mouth of God"** (Matt. 4:4).

Paul said we are to "learn not to go beyond the things which are written" (1 Cor. 4:6). Why? Because the things that are written (i.e. Scripture) are authoritative. In 1 Cor. 14:37 Paul wrote, "If any man thinketh himself to be a prophet, or spiritual, let him take knowledge of the things that I write you, that they are the commandment of the Lord." What is written in Scripture is binding and authoritative. Jesus said, **"He that rejecteth me, and receiveth not my sayings hath one that judgeth him: the word that I spake, the same shall judge him in the last day"** (John 12:48). The apostle John gave us an important warning in the book of Revelation. He said, **"The dead were judged out of the things which were written in the books, according to their works"** (Rev. 20:12). The "books" are the books of the Bible. Since the written word is authoritative and will judge us on the last day, we need to read it and study it diligently and obey it! Failure to do so is foolishness (cf. Matt. 7:24-27).

Conclusion

The majority of people go through life confused about ethics and morals. They constantly stumble their way through life, making wrong choices with terrible consequences. They do not have Scripture as their guide for ethical decisions. Paul said, **"And now I commend you to God, and the word of his grace, which is able to build you up, and to give you the inheritance among all them that are sanctified"** (Acts 20:32). The word of God can take us to heaven. It is our guide book. It is what we live by (Matt. 4:4). It tells us how to live on this earth to be pleasing to God Almighty. It is the standard by which all ethical and moral decisions are to be made. By it we will be judged and held accountable when we die. Therefore, we need to be good, serious-minded Bible students. There is absolutely no substitute for intense serious-minded Bible study!

For Thought or Discussion

1 Define "Christian ethics."
2 How are Christians not to live and to live?
3 How are Christians to walk? (Eph. 4:1; Col. 1:10; 1 Thess. 2:12)
4 Discuss one being "born a bad seed." Do you agree or disagree? Why?
5 Discuss feelings as an authority in ethics/morals.
6 What does Proverbs 14:12 teach?
7 (T or F) Our conscience determines truth.
8 What is similar about Paul's and Naaman's thinking?
9 (T or F) The basis for all ethical decisions is inside man.
10 (T or F) We are to lean upon our own thinking.
11 What is one who trusts in his own heart?
12 What is coming upon those who are prudent in their own sight?
13 How many will enter heaven? (Matthew 7:13-14) Do you agree? Why?
14 What did William Schulz say? Do you agree?
15 Who does Satan use to do his evil work?
16 What is the significance of 2 Timothy 3:16-17?
17 What did Paul say in 1 Cor. 4:6 and 1 Cor. 14:37?
18 What will judge us on the last day? (John 12:48)
19 How were the dead judged from Revelation 20:12?
20 Based on Matthew 7:24-27 how is one "wise" or "foolish'?
21 What are we to live by? Scripture?

Chapter 2-Holiness

Our songs in worship are designed to instruct as well as to praise. Paul said, "Let the word of Christ dwell in you richly; in all wisdom teaching and admonishing one another with psalms and hymns and spiritual songs, singing with grace in your hearts unto God" (Col. 3:16). Notice that our songs can teach and admonish and instruct! One familiar song with an important message is: "Take Time To Be Holy." Let us examine the song and the concept of holiness.

Defining the Word "Holy"

The Hebrew words *qadosh* "holy" and *qodesh* "holiness" occur more than 830 times in the Old Testament. The Greek word for "holy" is *hagios* and is used 229 times in the New Testament. Wycliffe states, "Obscure in etymology, the root idea of the Hebrew word, religiously viewed, is that of withdrawal and consecration: withdrawal from what is common or unclean, consecration to what is divine, sacred, pure." Wycliffe states again that these words "mean basically separation from what is common or unclean, and consecration to God (Lev. 20:24-26) . . . the underlying idea of apartness or separation from the profane (Lev. 10:10; Ezek. 22:26)." *Holman's Bible Dictionary* says the word holy is "a characteristic unique to God's nature which becomes the goal for human moral character. The idea of 'holy' is important for an understanding of God, of worship, and of the people of God in the Bible." Holman says the most important distinct meaning of holy is "to be set apart." The *Illustrated Dictionary of the Bible* defines holy as "moral and ethical wholeness or perfection; freedom from moral evil. Holiness is one of the essential elements of God's nature required of His people. Holiness may also be rendered 'sanctification' or 'godliness.' The word holy denotes that which is 'sanctified' or 'set apart' for divine service." The *Interpreter's Dictionary of the Bible* says concerning the word holy "the meaning of separation is paramount."

God Is Holy—We Are To Be Holy

Before we were ever born, God had determined that His people were to be holy, since He **"hath chosen us in him (i.e. Christ) before the foundation of the world, that we should be holy and without blemish before him in love"** (Eph. 1:4). Psalms 111:9 states, "Holy and reverend is his name." Joshua said, "For he is a holy God" (Josh. 24:19). Many times in the Old Testament God is called "the Holy One of Israel" (Isa. 5:24; Psa. 71:22; 2 Kings 19:22). God told the children of Israel, **"Ye shall be holy; for I Jehovah your God am holy"** (Lev. 19:2). This same teaching is found in Leviticus 11:44; 20:7-8, 22-26. Peter wrote, **"But like as he who called you is holy, be ye yourselves also holy in all manner of living; because it is written, Ye shall be holy; for I am holy"** (1 Pet. 1:15-16). Christians are described as a "holy priesthood" (1 Pet. 2:5) and a "holy nation" (1 Pet. 2:9). Exodus 15:11 states, "Who is like unto thee, O Jehovah, among the gods? Who is like unto thee, glorious in holiness, fearful in praises, doing wonders?" In Exodus 19:6 God demanded that His people be a "holy nation." Hannah prayed, "There is none holy as Jehovah; For there is none besides thee" (1

Sam. 2:2). Three times in the short Psalm 99 the repetition is thundered: "God is holy." In Isaiah 57:15 God declares His name "is holy." In Isaiah 6:3 one of the seraphim cried, "Holy, holy, holy is Jehovah of hosts." In Revelation 4:8 the four living creatures state, "Holy, holy, holy, is the Lord God, the Almighty, who was and who is and who is to come." The song of the victorious in heaven is: "for thou only art holy" (Rev. 15:4).

The Hebrew writer said without holiness **"no man shall see the Lord"** (KJV-Heb. 12:14). If we want to go to heaven, we must live holy lives. In view of the many wonderful promises we have received, Paul urges, "Let us cleanse ourselves from every defilement of flesh and spirit, perfecting holiness in the fear of the Lord" (2 Cor. 7:1). To be holy means to be set apart from sin and sanctified for God's use. It suggests living a life of purity and freedom from sin. Paul told Timothy, "Keep thyself pure" (1 Tim. 5:22). Our life of holiness begins at conversion when we are washed and sanctified and justified in the name of the Lord Jesus Christ (1 Cor. 6:11; Rom. 6:17-18). Because the world will be burned up and dissolved one day, Peter states, **"Seeing that these things are thus all to be dissolved. What manner of persons ought ye to be in all holy living and godliness"** (2 Pet. 3:11). Paul said, **"For God hath not called us unto uncleanness, but unto holiness"** (1 Thess. 4:7 KJV)

The goal of Christians is to grow into God's likeness (1 Pet. 1:15). Paul said, "Be ye therefore imitators of God, as beloved children" (Eph. 5:1). Jesus said, "Ye therefore shall be perfect, as your heavenly Father is perfect" (Matt. 5:48). Holiness of heart and life cannot be attained instantly, rather it is reached by years of diligent, patient effort (2 Pet. 3:18). It needs to repeated—**if the life of Jesus is not our pattern, the death of Jesus will not be our pardon.**

Biblical Examples

In Leviticus 10:1-2 we read, "And Nadab and Abihu, the sons of Aaron, took each of them his censer, and put fire thereon, and offered strange fire before Jehovah, which he not commanded them. And there came forth fire from before Jehovah, and devoured them, and they died before Jehovah." The word "strange" means "unlawful." Owens defines the Hebrew word as "unholy." Notice carefully verse three. Leviticus 10:3 says, "Then Moses said unto Aaron, This is it that Jehovah spake, saying, I will be sanctified in them that come nigh unto me, and before all the people I will be glorified." The word "sanctified" means "to be set apart or declare as holy." Through their disobedience Nadab and Abihu were not recognizing God's holiness. Through this account God is teaching Israel that His holiness will be honored! This is not a trivial thing. There will be serious consequences to those who fail to honor God as holy.

In Numbers 20:1-13 we have the account of the sin of Moses. Moses was told by Jehovah God to "speak" to the rock, and water would come forth. Moses disobeyed God and "smote the rock." Numbers 20:12 states, **"And Jehovah said unto Moses and Aaron, Because ye believed not in me, to sanctify me in the eyes of the children of Israel, therefore ye shall not bring this assembly into the land which I have given them."**

Moses did not "sanctify" God at Meribah. Moses disobeyed God and failed to honor God's holiness. The consequence of his sin was that he was not allowed to go into the promised land.

In Numbers 4:15 we read, "They shall not touch the sanctuary (i.e. the ark of the covenant), lest they die." The priests were instructed to carry the ark on long poles (Exodus 25:10-22). In 2 Samuel 6 they are carrying the ark on a "new cart." The cart starts to fall and Uzzah puts his hand forth to stop it from falling. God struck him dead there for his "error" (ASV margin--rashness; NKJV margin—irreverence). Uzzah's act was irreverent because he failed to obey the clear and plain teaching of Numbers 4:15. Uzzah did not sanctify God. He failed to honor the holiness of God.

We Must Take Time To Be Holy

The second verse of the song "Take Time To Be Holy" says, "The world rushes on." We live in a fast-paced world. Our lives are filled with activities that consume our time. My grandmother said many times, "You turn around and you have had a life." How true! James says our lives are like a "vapor" (Jam. 4:13-14). Twice Peter said we are only here "a little while" (1 Pet. 1:6; 5:10). Paul said we are only here "for the moment" (2 Cor. 4:17). Moses wrote, "The days of our years are threescore and ten, or even by reason of strength fourscore years" (Psa. 90:10). The lesson from this verse is given in Psalms 90:12, **"So teach us to number our days, that we may get us a heart of wisdom."**

Holiness must be pursued (Heb. 12:14). Holiness must be perfected (2 Cor. 7:1). Holiness is the fruit of service to God (Rom. 6:22). Paul said, **"Come ye out from among them, and be ye separate"** (2 Cor. 6:17). Peter said that we are "a people for God's own possession, that ye may show forth the excellencies of him who called you out of darkness into his marvelous light" (1 Pet. 2:9).

If we are not careful, time to develop holiness will be gone. So, we must take time to be holy. It must be a priority in our lives!

How Do We Take Time To Be Holy?

First, we must be a people of prayer. Notice the first verse says, "Speak oft with thy Lord" and "Forgetting in nothing His blessings to seek." The second verse says "Spend much time in secret with Jesus alone." Paul said, "Pray without ceasing" (1 Thess. 5:17) and "Continue steadfastly in prayer" (Col. 4:2). When we study the life of Jesus, we see Jesus constantly praying. We are told to be like Him (1 John 2:6). We are told to walk in his steps (1 Pet. 2:21). Jesus gave two parables on prayer—The Parable of the Midnight Friend (Luke 11:5-10) and The Parable of the Importunate Widow (Luke 18:1-8). The theme of these parables is keep praying and never quit! In Matthew 7:7-11 Jesus motivates us to constantly pray. Notice Jesus said, **"If ye then, being evil, know how to give good gifts unto your children, how much more shall your Father who is in heaven give good things to them that ask him?"** God will help us if we ask Him!

Second, we must diligently study God's word. The first verse says, "Feed on His word." In John 17:17 Jesus said, **"Sanctify them in thy truth: thy word is truth."** We are sanctified or made holy by God's word. Jesus said, **"Man shall not live by bread alone, but by every word that proceedeth out of the mouth of God"** (Matt. 4:4). Psalms 119:9 states, **"Wherewith shall a young man cleanse his way? By taking heed thereto according to thy word."** Psalms 119:11 states, "Thy word have I laid up in my heart, that I might not sin against thee." Psalms 119:105 says, "Thy word is a lamp unto my feet, and light unto my path." Acts 20:32 clearly teaches that the word of God is our guide book to heaven. Paul said that God guides and leads us "through the word of God that worketh in you that believe" (1 Thess. 2:13). The apostle John attributed spiritual strength to young Christians because "the word of God abideth in you" (1 John 2:14). Hebrews 4:12 says, **"For the word of God is living, and active, and sharper than any two-edged sword."** Paul said, "The sword of the Spirit" is "the word of God" (Eph. 6:17). The one who meditates on the law of Jehovah day and night is "blessed" (Psa. 1:1-2).

Third, we must have strong Christian friends. The first verse says, "Make friends of God's children." It also says, "Thy friends in thy conduct His likeness shall see." Paul warns us, **"Be not deceived: Evil companionships corrupt good morals"** (1 Cor. 15:33). We need strong Christian friends to help us be holy. Proverbs 13:20 NKJV states, **"Walk with wise men, and thou shalt be wise; But the companion of fools will be destroyed."** Proverbs 27:17 says, "Iron sharpeneth iron; so a man sharpeneth the countenance of his friend." Our closest friends can either pull us up to make us better or pull us down to make us evil. We cannot choose our relatives, but we can choose our friends.

Fourth, we must help others. The first verse says, "Help those who are weak." It was said about Jesus that He "went about doing good" (Acts 10:38). Acts 20:35 states, **"In all things I gave you an example, that so laboring ye ought to help the weak, and to remember the words of the Lord Jesus, that he himself said, It is more blessed to give than to receive."** There are many blessed's in the Bible, but there is only one "more blessed," and it has to do with giving! Jehovah has promised that He will bless us if we give to the poor (Deut. 15:7-11). Paul wrote, "So then, as we have opportunity, let us work that which is good toward all men, and especially toward them that are of the household of the faith" (Gal. 6:10). God expects us **"to be rich in good works."** In so doing we "lay up in store . . . a good foundation against the time to come" (1 Tim. 6:17-19). Christians by their very nature should be **"zealous of good works"** (Tit. 3:14). Faithful disciples understand very clearly that **"faith apart from works is dead"** (Jam. 2:26).

Fifth, we must think good, positive, holy thoughts. The third verse says, "Each thought and each motive beneath His control." Sin starts in the heart. This is why Solomon says, **"Keep thy heart with all diligence; for out of it are the issues of life"** (Prov. 4:23). Proverbs 23:7 says, "For as he thinketh within himself, so is he." We are not what we think we are—rather we are what we think! Jesus said, "Blessed are the pure in heart for they shall see God" (Matt. 5:8). The formula for a pure heart is given in Philippians 4:8, "Whatsoever things are true, honorable, just, pure, lovely, and of good report; if there be any virtue . . . any praise, think on these things." Paul said, **"Bringing every thought into captivity to the obedience of Christ"** (2 Cor. 10:5).

Sixth, we must not love the world. The song ends with this phrase, "Thou soon shall be fitted for service above." One song says, "We are here just to learn to love Him, we'll be home in a little while." John wrote, **"Love not the world, neither the things that are in the world. If any man love the world, the love of the Father is not in him. For all that is in the world, the lust of the flesh and the lust of the eyes and the vainglory of life, is not of the Father, but is of the world. And the world passeth away, and the lust thereof: but he that doeth the will of God abideth for ever"** (1 John 2:15-17). Paul said, "Demas forsook me, having loved this present world" (2Tim. 4:10). For all eternity Demas will regret his bad decision. If we do the will of God, we will abide forever and will never regret our decision. Those who go to heaven—"loved not their life even unto death" (Rev. 12:11).

Seventh, we must be holy in our daily habits. The song says, "Abide in Him always." Paul wrote, **"Or know ye not that your body is a temple of the Holy Spirit which is in you, which ye have from God? And ye are not your own: for ye were bought with a price: glorify God therefore in your body"** (1Cor. 6:19-20). God expects us to glorify Him in our bodies. We should carefully watch over our eating habits, for gluttony is to be avoided (Prov. 23:21). Tobacco, alcoholic beverages, and illicit drugs need to be avoided. It is important to mention habits that we need: promptness, diligence, courtesy, cleanliness, and a multitude of other daily deeds. The way we behave ourselves will either cause men to glorify our Father who is in heaven or reject Him (Matt. 5:16). Christians are commanded to be "the salt of the earth" (Matt. 5:13). Paul said, **"Whether therefore ye eat, or drink, or whatsoever ye do, do all to the glory of God"** (1 Cor. 10:31).

The Blessings of Taking Time To Be Holy

The third verse says, "Be calm in thy soul." A faithful Christian can have **"the peace of God which passeth all understanding"** (Phil. 4:7). He can know he will receive the crown of life (Rev. 2:10; Jam. 1:12) and great reward in heaven (Matt. 5:12). Paul wrote, "For our light affliction, which is for the moment, worketh for us more and more exceedingly an eternal weight of glory" (2 Cor. 4:17). Again Paul said, "For I reckon that the sufferings of this present time are not worthy to be compared with the glory which shall be revealed to us-ward" (Rom. 8:18). Psalms 119:165 states, **"Great peace have they that love thy law."** When one loves, studies, meditates upon the word of God, he will be led in the right path and have great peace and calmness of soul.

The second verse says, "Like Him thou shalt be." Jesus said, "The disciple is not above his teacher: but every one when he is perfected shall be as his teacher" (Luke 6:40). The more we strive to be like Jesus, the more we will be like Him. A disciple is one who follows the teachings of Jesus.

The second verse also says, "Thy friends in thy conduct His likeness shall see." Acts 4:13 states, "Now when they beheld the boldness of Peter and John, and had perceived that they were unlearned and ignorant men, they marveled; and they took knowledge of them, that they had been with Jesus." The boldness of Jesus had been transferred to Peter and John. Because they had been with Jesus, they had been transformed.

The third verse says, "Thou soon shall be fitted for service above." Revelation 7:15 states, "Therefore are they before the throne of God: and they serve him day and night in his temple."

Conclusion

Christians are to be "holy, and without blemish" (Eph. 5:27), and the main way we can do this is by the process of separating ourselves from the world (2 Cor. 6:17-18). We are in the world, but we are not to be of the world (John 17:14-16). We need to take time to be holy. To be holy takes time, effort, desire, perseverance, and a mind-set to be holy like God is holy. May this song always remind us of the need to slow down to do those things that are so crucial to our spiritual growth.

For Thought or Discussion

1 What are two key concepts within our songs?
2 Define the Hebrew word *qadosh*.
3 What did Holman say about the word "holy"?
4 What command is given in Leviticus 19:2?
5 Is this command given in the New Testament? If so, where?
6 What does Isaiah 6:3 and Revelation 4:8 state?

7   What does Hebrews 12:14 (KJV) teach?

8   What is Peter's argument in 2 Peter 3:11?

9   What does Ephesians 5:1 teach? Matthew 5:48?

10 Define the word "strange" in Leviticus 10:1.

11 What did God say in Leviticus 10:3?

12 How did Moses fail to "sanctify" God at Meribah?

13 How is Uzzah's sin characterized? Why?

14 What is the lesson we can learn from Psalms 90:10, 12?

15 What are seven ways we must pursue holiness?

16 What did Jesus teach in Matthew 7:7-11?

17 From John 17:17 how are we sanctified?

18 What does Proverbs 13:20 teach?

19 What is significant about the phrase "more blessed"?

20 Discuss Proverbs 23:7.

21 What did Demas do wrong?

22 From Matthew 5:16 how do we glorify God?

23 What is promised to the faithful Christian in the next life?

24 What will one receive who loves the law?

25 From Matthew 5:13-16 what two things are Christians to be?

Chapter 3-Sexual Ethics

The apostle Paul stated, **"For the grace of God hath appeared, bringing salvation to all men, instructing us, to the intent that, denying ungodliness and worldly lusts, we should live soberly and righteously and godly in this present world"** (Titus 2:11-12). An integral part of having and living a high Christian ethic is that we deny ourselves ungodliness and worldly lusts and that we live soberly and righteously and godly in this present world! When Paul gives his list of sins in 1 Cor. 5:9-11; 1 Cor. 6:9-11; Gal. 5:19-22; Eph. 5:3-4; and Col. 3:5, what sin is listed first on the list? The answer is: "fornication."

In Ephesians 5:5 we read, **"For this ye know of a surety, that no fornicator . . . hath any inheritance in the kingdom of Christ and God."** Paul also said, **"For this is the will of God, even your sanctification, that ye abstain from fornication; that each one of you know how to possess himself of his own vessel in sanctification and honor, not in the passion of lust, even as the Gentiles who know not God"** (1 Thess. 4:3-5). In Ephesians 5:3 we read, "Fornication . . . let it not even be named among you, as becometh saints." John wrote, "Fornicators . . . their part shall be in the lake that burneth with fire and brimstone; which is the second death" (Rev. 21:8). Therefore, it becomes absolutely essential that we take this sin very seriously. This is no trivial matter.

The Definition of Fornication

The word "fornication" comes from the Greek word *porneia*. John Stott defines the word as "physical sexual immorality." Zodhiates says it is a broad word that means "to commit fornication or any sexual sin" (*The Complete Word Study Dictionary*). Thayer defines the word to include any form of "illicit sexual intercourse-adultery, fornication, homosexuality, lesbianism, etc." Moulton and Milligan state it "came to be applied to unlawful sexual intercourse generally."

The Sexual Problem We Face Today

Today, more than ever, we are plagued with sexual problems. Sadly, the Church of our Lord has not escaped these problems. Many people are increasingly engaging in illicit sex with disastrous results—illegitimate births, sexually–transmitted diseases, hurt feelings, destroyed lives, divorce, and even murder. In 1978, eighty percent of American college students in a survey said pre-marital sex was all right on the first date. More and more unmarried couples are "shacking up" and living together. In 1984, *The Dallas Morning News* had an article entitled "More Americans Than Ever Are Having Affairs." In 1997, one study estimated that 50 percent of teenagers 16-19 were having sex. Some say that monogamy is not working (consider the divorce rate) therefore, open and free love is to be preferred over a monogamous marriage. Many people see nothing wrong with sex outside of marriage. In fact, some people think it would be beneficial. On national television one Ph.D. said,

"Sexual indulgence is a marital glue to save marriages."
Isaiah said long ago, however, **"Woe unto them that
call evil good, and good evil; that put darkness for
light, and light for darkness; that out bitter for sweet,
and sweet for bitter!"** (Isa. 5:20).

Dr. Nancy Clatworthy, sociology professor at Ohio
State, did a study of couples living together before
marriage. Before the study, she thought living together
before marriage would be a beneficial step in the
courtship process. However, she concluded her study by
saying, "Living together is not a good prelude to
marriage." Regardless of what some sociology professor
says, the most important thing is what God says!

Listen carefully to what a high school girl wrote:

"I am a high school girl who believes in free love.
There are plenty more like me. I am not a
pushover. I come from a high class family and I
make good grades. I see nothing wrong with
sleeping with different boys so long as I like them
and they like me-as a person, I mean. Virginity is
an old-fashioned idea that makes no sense
anymore. Why should a girl save herself for a man
who is not making any great effort to save himself
for her? In our social group I don't know of a
single guy who has done much of a preservation
job. Sex is an important part of marriage, and I
want to be the perfect wife. The practice I am
getting now will be very useful when Mr. Right
comes along. So you see, there are logical and
sensible arguments against virginity."

One fourteen-year-old girl said, "If you don't get pregnant, I don't see any harm in it." An unmarried eighteen-year-old girl, pregnant, wrote to her parents, "I just feel that sex cannot be wrong if it is with someone you truly do love." Notice that the basis for her judgment was her feelings. But, feelings do not determine right or wrong—God's word does! We are to live by the word of God (Matt. 4:4), not our feelings. This girl was leaning upon her own understanding as opposed to God's revealed word (Prov. 3:5-6; 28:26; Jer. 10:23). Big sin! Big mistake! Debbie Boone sang a song entitled "You Light Up My Life." In the song she says, "It can't be wrong when it feels so right." Yes, it can! Feelings do not determine right and wrong.

In the 1960's there was a song called "Sweet Cream Ladies." This song openly glorified the prostitute and that the prostitute was performing a valuable service to the men of America. One study in the 1990's revealed that one out of every seven men has gone to a prostitute. If the prostitute is unrepentant, she is taking herself to an eternal hell of fire (Rev. 21:8). If the men who gave her business are unrepentant, they will also suffer the same fate (Rom. 2:5-9). The morality of America is in trouble. Christians must stand and oppose this ungodliness and live soberly and righteously and godly!

The Ungodly Influence of Margaret Sanger

Margaret Sanger founded and provided the philosophical basis for Planned Parenthood. This is an organization that has promoted the abortion of millions of unborn human beings. She has been instrumental in promoting the revolution aimed at breaking down the family and establishing a free-love ethic in its place. Elasah Drogin wrote, "If it is possible for one person to change the very foundations of civilization from a moral one to an immoral one, then Margaret Sanger should rightfully be known as the founder of modern culture because today's culture is characterized precisely by the values she and her admirers taught." A goal of Planned Parenthood was candidly to help "young people obtain sex satisfaction before marriage. By sanctioning sex before marriage, we will prevent fear and guilt." Sanger denounced marriage as "a degenerate institution" and sexual modesty as "obscene prudery." She told her husband that she wanted liberation from the bonds of marriage and deserted him to practice free love.

The Devastation of Sexual Immorality

Sexual immorality destroys the body through bacterial STDs (Chlamydia, Syphilis, Gonorrhea) and through viral STDs (Genital Herpes, Hepatitis B, AIDS- which are incurable). Paul said, **"Flee fornication, every sin that a man doeth is without the body; but he that commiteth fornication sinneth against his own body"** (1 Cor. 6:18). Fornication will cause one to mourn at his latter end when his flesh and body are consumed (Prov. 5:11).

Sexual immorality destroys the home. Marriage is intended for life, but because of lust and a free-love ethic, a home is destroyed. The children of a broken home are devastated with emotional and psychological effects that last forever. Those who engage in adultery don't stop and consider what they are doing to their children.

Sexual immorality destroys one's influence. One man who committed adultery recognized that he will never again be the man his son can look up to with respect, and his daughter will never see him again as the apple of her eye. Proverbs 6:33 states, **"Wounds and dishonor shall he get; and his reproach shall not be wiped away."**

Sexual immorality destroys one's soul. A person who commits fornication "wrongeth his own soul" (Prov. 8:36). Proverbs 6:32 says, **"He that commiteth adultery with a woman is void of understanding: He that doeth it who would destroy his own soul."** Sadly, unrepentant fornicators are going to hell (Eph. 5:5; Rev. 21:8; Heb. 12:14; Gal. 5:19-22).

There Is No Sin in Being Tempted

We must understand that there is no sin in being tempted. Jesus was tempted to sin but never did (Heb. 4:15). We sing the song: "Yield Not To Temptation" for yielding is sin." How true! When we yield to the temptation, we sin! There is pleasure in sin (Heb. 11:25), but the pleasure is only momentary. We must remember the pleasure of the sin is not worth the punishment and chastisement that will certainly come upon the sinner (Rom. 2:5-11). Proverbs 9:17-18 states, "Stolen waters are sweet, and bread eaten in secret is pleasant. But he knoweth not that the dead are there; that her guests are in the depths of Sheol." Notice that stolen waters are sweet. In other words, one will enjoy the pleasure of the sin. But, the end result of engaging in the sin will be heartache and destruction. The pleasure of the sin will not be worth the suffering that God imposes on us. We will forever regret our bad choice. Therefore, let us be wise and refuse to yield to the temptation (Prov. 12:15).

We Must Guard Our Hearts

Proverbs 4:23 states **"Keep thy heart with all diligence; for out of it are the issues of life."** Jesus said, "For out of the abundance of the heart the mouth speaketh" (Matt. 12:34). Jesus is teaching that what we say and do comes from the condition and attitude of our heart. But, our heart is determined by what we think. Proverbs 23:7 says, **"For as a man thinketh within himself, so is he."** We are not what we think we are, rather we are what we think! We must make a commitment to guard our hearts. Daniel 1:8 states, "But Daniel purposed in his heart that he would not defile himself." This was the key. We cannot wait until the temptation comes. We have to make a commitment in advance. When Potiphar's wife tempted Joseph to lie with her (i.e. commit adultery), he said, **"How then can I do this great wickedness, and sin against God?"** (Gen. 39:9). Notice that Joseph understood that sexual immorality was a sin against God. Before the temptation came, he had purposed in his heart not to sin! We must do likewise.

When David saw Bathsheba bathing she "was very beautiful to look upon" (2 Sam. 11:2). Not just "beautiful" but "very beautiful." Certainly this increased the temptation. When David found out that Bathsheba was "the wife of Uriah the Hittite," that should have ended the matter. But David went full-steam ahead to gratify the lust of the flesh. He committed the sins of coveting, stealing, drunkenness, adultery, and murder.

God pronounced a fourfold punishment upon David that was very painful and not worth the few minutes of pleasure he got from his sin. The wise Christian will deny himself the temporary pleasures of sin; he will obey God and look forward to an eternal home in heaven (Titus 2:12-14; 2 Cor. 4:17; Rom. 8:18; Heb. 11:24-26).

The Importance of the Word of God

John wrote, **"Ye are strong, and the word of God abideth in you"** (1 John 2:14). When Jesus was tempted to sin, every time He said, "It is written." If Jesus, the Son of God, used the written word of God to defeat Satan's temptations, what does that say to you and me? We are to do likewise (1 Pet. 2:21; 1 John 2:6). John also wrote, **"This is the victory that hath overcome the world, even our faith"** (1 John 5:4). But, Romans 10:17 states, **"Faith cometh by hearing, and hearing by the word of God."** If we want a strong faith, we must firmly establish the word of God in our hearts (Psa. 119:11, 105). Twice in Ephesians 6, Paul instructs us to put on the whole armor of God. Every part of the armor is related to the word of God. The reason for doing this is that we "may be able to stand against the wiles of the devil" (Eph. 6:11). Paul said, **"And now I commend you to God, and to the word of his grace, which is able to build you up, and to give you the inheritance among all them that are sanctified"** (Acts 20:32). Jesus said, **"Man shall live not by bread alone, but by every word that proceedeth out of the mouth of God"** (Matt. 4:4).

God's Plan To Prevent Sexual Immorality

God made Adam and Eve as sexual human beings with sexual needs. We have nothing to be ashamed of for having the desire to have sex. But, God has placed a fence around approved sex—and that fence is marriage! Other people may laugh at us and scorn us for teaching this, but this is the Christian sexual ethic. Hebrews 13:4 states, **"Let marriage be had in honor among all, and let the bed be undefiled: for fornicators and adulterers God will judge."** The word "bed" in Greek is the word *koite* which means "marital relationship; sexual intercourse." God's word clearly teaches that sex in marriage is honorable and undefiled. Outside of marriage sex is sinful and damnable. Paul wrote, "But, because of fornications, let each man have his own wife, and let each woman have her own husband" (1 Cor. 7:2). The plural word "fornications" is the Greek *porneias* which means "the many temptations to sexual immorality." Paul clearly teaches in 1 Corinthians 7:1-5 that the way to prevent sexual immorality is for husband and wife to meet each other's sexual needs. A Christian spouse must not "defraud" their mate (i.e. withhold sex) unless it is by "consent." And then it can only be for a "season" (i.e. a predetermined time set—e.g. one month or whatever time is agreed upon). Christians need to realize that marital sex is an important way to build more love into your marriage.

Proverbs 5:15-23 teaches God-approved sex is between a husband and his wife. Verse 15 states, **"Drink waters out of thine own cistern, and running waters out of thine own well."** The husband is instructed to go his wife and his wife alone for his sexual needs. Verse

19 states, "Let her breasts satisfy thee at all times." Notice "her breasts." This implies that the wife must respond by allowing her husband to have access to her body. If a husband goes to another woman for sex, it is **"iniquity"** and **"sin"** (verse 22). If a husband goes to another woman, he will **"die"** and his actions are called **"folly"** (verse 23).

A Sad True Story

Several years ago a preacher came to me with a very serious problem. His Christian wife was sexually defrauding him. Sadly, I learned from others that because his wife was defrauding him, he was having sex with another woman. While we can sympathize with him and some can even empathize, her sin did not give him permission to go outside the marriage relationship to fulfill his sexual needs (Rom. 3:8). While it will be hard and difficult, a Christian in this situation must be faithful and not commit adultery. He needs to realize he will be rewarded for his faithfulness (Rev. 2:10; Jam. 1:12; 2 Cor. 4:17; Rom. 8:18). He needs to ask the Lord to help him (Phil. 4:19; Matt. 7:7-11).

Integrity

The following account is based on a true story. A millionaire took a girl on a date. He asked her, "If I gave you a million dollars, would you go to bed with me tonight?" She thought to herself—well, I know he has the money, and just think what I could do with a million dollars! So she said "yes." After a minute or so, the millionaire asked her, "If I were to give you ten thousand dollars, would you go to bed with me tonight?" Again she thought—well, ten thousand is not a million, but it is still a lot of money. I could do a lot with ten thousand dollars! So she said "yes." After another minute went by, the millionaire asked her, "If I were to give you one hundred dollars, would you go to bed with me?" She became indignant and responded, "Wait just a minute. What do you think I am?" He said, "We've already determined that. We're just trying to fix a price." The lesson is that money has nothing to do with morality. The price of one dollar would be just as wrong as a million dollars. Christian ethics would say it is sinful regardless of the price.

Conclusion

Even though many people are living together unmarried, the Christian sexual ethic is to teach that such behavior is sinful. The Christian sexual ethic is to **"abstain from fornication"** (1 Thess. 4:3) and **"flee fornication"** (1 Cor. 6:18). The Christian ethic is to teach that God has placed a fence around sex and that fence is marriage! Inside that fence it is God-approved and holy and undefiled, but outside of that fence it is sin and damnable (Heb. 13:4). Sexual immorality is too serious to take lightly. It can destroy the body and home and most importantly one's eternal soul. Forgiveness is possible, but the consequences of sin are not erased. **"His reproach shall not be wiped away"** (Prov. 6:33).

For Thought or Discussion

1 What did Paul say Christians are to deny?
2 How are Christians to live in this present world?
3 What did Paul teach about fornication?
4 Define "fornication."

5 What are the consequences of illicit sex?

6 (T or F) Monogamy is not working so free love is acceptable.

7 (T or F) Sexual indulgence is a marital glue to save marriages.

8 Discuss the high school girl who believes in sex before marriage.

9 (T or F) Feelings determine truth.

10 What did the song "Sweet Cream Ladies" teach?

11 What is a goal of Planned Parenthood?

12 What are four things sexual immorality destroys?

13 (T or F) We sin when we are tempted.

14 (T or F) There is pleasure in sin. Scripture?

15 What will a wise Christian do when tempted to sin?

16 How did Daniel not defile himself? (Daniel 1:8)

17 What two things did Joseph call adultery?

18 What are five sins David committed in the Bathsheba story?

19 What did Jesus say every time He was tempted?

20 How do we obtain a strong faith?

21 What are Christians to live by? (Matt. 4:4)

22 (T or F) Sexual desire is sinful.

23 What is the fence God has placed around sex?

24 Define the word "fornications" in 1 Cor 7:2?

25 Define the word "defraud" in 1 Corinthians 7:5?

26 What does "Drink waters out of thine own cistern" mean in context?

27 What is the significance of "her breasts" in Proverbs 5:19?

28 Describe the husband who commits adultery from Proverbs 5:22-23.

29 What do you think about the "Sad True Story?"

Chapter 4- Homosexuality

America is being bombarded with the problem of homosexuality. Today it is a volatile and politically-charged issue. It has become more prevalent to view homosexuality as an acceptable, alternative lifestyle. In some areas equal rights are being granted to practice and promote this lifestyle. There are now gay churches, even gay priests and ministers in mainstream denominations. Some vacation resorts often cater to the open display of homosexual behavior. This is certainly a moral issue that confronts the Church of our Lord today! Some Christians question whether it is wrong while others react in ways unbecoming of a Christian.

Walter Barnett, a homosexual, wrote, "Some theologians and a number of gay Christians, working from a growing understanding of the biblical texts, have come to the conclusion that the Bible does not exclude homosexual people from the Christian fellowship" (*Homosexuality and the Bible*, p. 3). John J. McNeill, a homosexual, stated, "Nowhere in the Scripture is there a clear condemnation of a loving sexual relationship between two gay persons" (*Homosexuality: Challenging the Church to Grow*, p. 246). Are these claims correct? As with any moral/ethical issue, we must examine the word of God to find the truth!

Homosexuality in the Patriarchal Age

Homosexuality led to the destruction of Sodom and Gomorrah. Jehovah God said, **"Their sin is very grievous"** (Gen. 18:20). The men of the city, both young and old, were involved (Gen. 19:4-5). The text says "the men of Sodom" wanted to "know" the two men (angels) that were in Lot's house. The word "know" (Heb. *yada;* Grk. *ginosko*) is sometimes used in the Bible as a euphemism for "to know in a sexual way" or "to have sexual relations with" (cf. Gen. 4:1; Matt. 1:25). Lot begs the men of Sodom "Do not so wickedly" (Gen. 19:7). This teaches very clearly that homosexuality is wickedness. God destroyed the cities with "brimstone and fire" because of their sin (Gen. 19:15, 24 and 2 Pet. 2:6-8). Jude 7 gives an inspired commentary on the problem. Jude 7 states, **"Sodom and Gomorrah . . . had given themselves over to fornication and gone after strange flesh, are set forth as an example, suffering the punishment of eternal fire."** Could this be plainer? Homosexuals will suffer the punishment of an eternal hell of fire. There are two ways homosexuals argue against this Genesis 19 passage. First, they say the sin in the Lot-angels story was not homosexuality but homosexual rape, and rape is always wrong. The problem with that view is that it was pronounced before Genesis 19 that **"their sin is very grievous."** Plus, what does the word "sodomite" mean? It means "sexual intercourse between two male persons." Second, they say Lot was guilty of a violation of the hospitality code. They say since he was an alien, his visitors should have had their credentials examined by the Sodomites. This argument just does not hold water! It is ridiculous. The bottom line is homosexuality was and is a **"very grievous"** sin!

Homosexuality in the Mosaic Age

Leviticus 18:22 states, **"Thou shalt not lie with mankind, as with womankind: It is abomination."** Homosexuality was a reason the other nations were driven out (Lev. 18:24-25). The Israelites were warned in Leviticus 18:26-30 that they would be driven out if they defiled the land with these "abominations" (e.g. homosexuality). Leviticus 20:13 states, **"And if a man lie with mankind, as with womankind, both of them have committed abomination: they shall surely be put to death; their blood shall be upon them."** We need to remember that Jesus lived under the Law of Moses. It did not end until His death on the cross (Col. 2:14). While it was in force, Jesus taught strict observance of the Law of Moses (Matt. 5:17-20). Therefore, Jesus approved of what the Law of Moses taught about homosexuality. Deuteronomy 23:17 states, **"There shall be no prostitute of the daughters of Israel, neither shall there be a sodomite of the sons of Israel."** Homosexuals say in these verses that homosexuality is condemned only when it is associated with idolatrous, pagan rites. This is twisting and perverting Scripture to one's own destruction (2 Pet. 3:15-17).

Homosexuality in the Christian Age

Paul wrote, **"For this cause God gave them up unto vile passions: for their women changed the natural use into that which is against nature: and likewise also the men, leaving the natural use of the**

woman, burned in their lust one toward another, men
with men working unseemliness, and receiving in
themselves that recompense of their error which was
due" (Rom. 1:26-27). Notice carefully homosexuality is
called "vile passions" and "error" and "leaving the
natural use of the woman." Homosexuals reinterpret
this passage to teach that Paul is condemning unnatural
homosexual actions (Sherwin Bailey, *Homosexuality and
the Western Christian Tradition*, pp. 1-28). This is
sometimes called the "abuse argument." They say Paul
only condemns homosexual acts committed by
apparently heterosexual persons and heterosexual acts
committed by homosexuals. Again, they are twisting and
perverting Scripture unto their own destruction. Chris
Glaser, a homosexual, wrote, "Clearly, Paul is wrong.
Reason and experience (and science their product)
contradict his understanding. We cannot be saved by
behaving heterosexually, only by following Christ.
Christ Jesus, give us the faith to follow you, rather than
the idolatrous god of heterosexuality." It is the height of
absolute heresy and total foolishness to say "Paul is
wrong." Glaser just denies what Paul taught. Paul said
that what he wrote is "the commandment of the Lord" (1
Cor. 14:37). Jesus endorsed the apostles (Matt. 16:18;
18:18; Luke 10:16; John 13:20) and Peter endorsed the
writings of Paul as Scripture (2 Pet. 3:15-17). Jesus said,
"The scripture cannot be broken" (John 10:35).
Therefore, a failure to accept what Paul wrote is a failure
to follow Jesus! Sadly, Glaser does not know this.
Glaser is wrong, not Paul!

In 1 Corinthians 6:9-11 Paul says, **"Or know ye not . . . that homosexuals . . . shall not inherit the kingdom of God."** In 1Timothy 1:8-10 Paul says that homosexuality is "contrary to the sound doctrine." Homosexuals say the meaning of the Greek word *arsenokoitai* in these verses is uncertain. They say it is unwise to use an uncertain word to condemn homosexuality. Therefore, it is imperative that we closely examine the Greek word translated "homosexuals."

The Eight Major English Translations of *arsenokoitai*—

KJV—abusers of themselves with mankind; NKJV—homosexuals; ASV—abusers of themselves with men; NASV—homosexuals; RSV—homosexuals; NRSV—sodomites; NIV—homosexual offenders; ESV—men who practice homosexuality

Greek Lexicons and their definition of *arsenokoitai*—

Thayer—one who lies with a male as with a female, a sodomite; *Arndt and Gingrich*—a male who practices homosexuality, sodomite; *Zodhiates*—a man who lies in bed with another male, a homosexual; *Abbott-Smith*—sodomite; The *Analytical Greek Lexicon*—one who lies with a male, a sodomite; *UBS NT Greek Dictionary*—male sexual pervert; *Dictionary of NT Theology*—includes sins as homosexuality

The Greek word *arsenokoitai* is from two Greek words—*arsen* (male) and *koite* (bed). Literally, the word means males in bed with males! The conclusion of this word study is the meaning of the Greek word is not uncertain! The Greek word means homosexuals— period. Greek scholarship is united and clear! Homosexuals do not want to believe that the word means homosexuals so they believe false doctrine. They do not believe the truth because they do not want truth. They are looking for any way to justify their damnable practices.

What Causes Homosexuality?

Some homosexuals say, "God made me this way." But, God does not make one a homosexual and then condemn him to hell because he is a homosexual. That is nonsense which puts God at fault which is absurd (Job 40:8). There has been no definitive study proving homosexuality is genetic. Since God has given people reproductive organs, He made them for heterosexual relationships. The fact that some homosexuals have turned to heterosexual relationships is a major problem for them. This proves that God did not make them homosexuals.

Dr. Michael Bailey of Northwestern University examined 110 pairs of identical twins who had been separated at birth and raised in different environments. He found that if one twin was gay, there was a 52% chance the other was, also. It is a known fact that identical twins are genetically alike. If homosexuality were genetic, they would have the same gender preference. The fact that 48% were not gay confirms genetics alone does not cause homosexuality.

There is no one definitive cause of a tendency to homosexuality. Some factors that may be involved are a melancholy temperament, a lack of healthy parental relationships (absent father, smother mother), a lack of physical expressions of love especially from the father when the child is young, and early exposure to improper sexual activity.

What About Same-Sex Marriages?

Marriage is a divine institution—not a civil one. God determines what constitutes a proper marriage—not men (Acts 5:29). Paul wrote, **"Let each man have his own wife, and let each woman have her own husband"** (1 Cor. 7:2). There is not one mention regarding same-sex marriage in the Bible. The practice was known among the Gentiles. The Roman Emperor Nero had two same-sex marriages (Pythagorus, Sporus). Marriage throughout the Bible is always between a man and a woman.

What Should Be a Christian's Response?

First, we must teach the truth of God's word. Paul said, "For I shrank not from declaring unto you the whole counsel of God" (Acts 20:27). We are told to imitate Paul (1 Cor. 11:1; 2 Thess. 2:15). We must teach sound doctrine which is according to the glorious gospel (1 Tim. 1:8-11). Peter said, **"We must obey God rather than men"** (Acts 5:29). It may be politically incorrect to teach homosexuality is a damnable sin, but we cannot compromise the truth of God's word! Sadly, homosexuals "glory in their shame" (Phil. 3:19).

Second, we must preach the truth in love (Eph. 4:15). Jesus taught we are to love our neighbor (Mark 12:31) and even love our enemies (Matt. 5:44). Paul said, "Bless them that persecute you; bless and curse not" (Rom. 12:14). Very simply we must hate the sin but love the sinner. In 2 Timothy 2:24-26 Paul instructed, "And the Lord's servant must not strive, but be gentle towards all, apt to teach, forbearing, in meekness correcting them that oppose themselves; if peradventure God may give them repentance unto the knowledge of the truth, and they may recover themselves out of the snare of the devil, having been taken captive by him unto his will." The Bible teaches us to count everyone a neighbor and to love our neighbors as ourselves. It requires us, even as we deal with conduct we believe to be sinful, to be gentle and humble, not arrogant or self-righteous. It forbids calling others obscene or offensive names or using violence.

Third, we must offer the hope of the gospel. We are saved through hope (Rom. 8:24-25). The gospel has facts to be believed (1 Cor. 15:1-4), commands to obeyed (John 8:24; Mark 16:15-16), promises to be enjoyed (Rev. 2:10; Jam. 1:12), and warnings to be heeded (Mark 16:15-15; 2 Thess. 1: 7-10). The gospel provides deliverance from sexual immorality.

A True Story

Several years ago the Bangs Church of Christ in Bangs, Texas decided to put on the marquee one sin each week from the list of sins in 1 Corinthians 6:9-11 that would cause one to "not inherit the kingdom of God." No one said anything until the church put the sin "homosexuals" on their marquee. The local newspapers attacked the church. The Church was accused of all kinds of hatred and bigotry. But, stop and think! The Bangs Church of Christ did not write the Bible! They were simply stating what the Bible clearly says! Sooner or later one must come to the understanding that the Bible is God's guide book to heaven (Matt. 4:4; Acts 20:32). If one gets angry at what the Bible teaches, their anger is really directed against God. 1 Samuel 12:9-10 teaches to despise the word of God is to despise God Himself.

Conclusion

In summary, the homosexuals' attempt to reinterpret Scripture is simply twisting, perverting, distorting, and wresting Scripture unto their own destruction (2 Pet. 3:15-17). They have failed miserably to give us the correct understanding. They are simply playing passover with Scripture. They pass over the real meaning. They have a preconceived opinion and go to the Bible to prove their point. They put on their rose-colored glasses and see what they want to see instead of the truth that unrepentant homosexuality is a sin that will keep people out of heaven. God made Adam and Eve not Adam and Steve. He also did not make Eve and Evelyn. Sexual relations between a husband and wife are "natural" (Rom. 1:27). Sexual relations between two men or two women are unnatural, sinful, and damnable. We did not write the Bible! When we stand for the truth, we should expect opposition. Jesus said, **"Woe unto you, when all men speak well of you!"** (Luke 6:26). The prophets were persecuted (Matt. 5:12). We will also suffer for standing for the truth (1 Pet. 4:12-16; 2 Tim. 3:12; John 15:20; Acts 14:22; Psa. 34:19).

For Thought or Discussion

1 Today what is the political attitude of people toward homosexuality?
2 What did Walter Barnett and John J. McNeill say?
3 Describe the sin of Sodom and Gomorrah.
4 Define the word "know" in Genesis 4:1; 19:5 and Matthew 1:25.
5 What proves that homosexuality is wickedness? (Genesis 18:20; 19:7)
6 How do homosexuals try to answer the Lot story?
7 What do Leviticus 18:22 and 20:13 clearly teach?
8 Discuss "the natural use of the woman" in Rom. 1.
9 (T or F) Three times in Romans 1:24-28 Paul says "God gave them up."
10 What did Chris Glaser say about Paul?
11 Prove the writings of Paul are endorsed by Jesus.
12 What does 1 Corinthians 6:9-11 teach?
13 How do homosexuals argue against 1 Corinthians 6:9-11?
14 Discuss the Greek word *arsenokoitai.*
15 (T or F) God makes one a homosexual.
16 What proves that one is not born a homosexual?
17 What are some possible causes of homosexuality?
18 What does 1 Corinthians 7:2 teach?
19 How should a Christian respond to homosexuality?
20 What do you think about what happened in Bangs?
21 Discuss "We did not write the Bible."
22 Prove that to despise the word of God is the same as despising God.

Chapter 5-Abortion

Abortion is a moral issue that confronts Christians and the world. Abortion is the gruesome termination of a pregnancy before birth, resulting in the death of the baby. Wikipedia states, "Around 56 million abortions are performed each year in the world." In 1996, there were 1.37 million abortions in the USA. The reason 93% women give for having an abortion is because the child is unwanted and inconvenient (cf. The Center for Bio-Ethical Reform). Yes, abortion is controversial, highly sensitive, debated, emotional, and even a political issue. But, our primary ethical concern about abortion involves the moral question—is it acceptable to God? The reader may already have his mind made up on this question. But, I urge you to have an open mind. Proverbs 18:13 states, **"He that giveth answer before he heareth it, it is folly and shame unto him."**

Background to the Abortion Issue

There was a time when politicians would not touch this abortion issue with a ten-foot pole. They said abortion is a moral and religious issue not a political one. They wanted to keep church and state separate. But now, because of the Women's Liberation Movement and Planned Parenthood, women are bringing this problem to the forefront. They are telling their congressmen: if you don't vote for abortion, we are not going to vote for you.

I do believe that Christians should be involved with politics. We ought to be concerned about the direction our country is headed. We ought to use every honest and legal way to stop wholesale abortion. Murdering doctors and bombing abortions clinics is ungodly and sinful. Paul asked the pointed question and then answered it! He asked, **"Let us do evil, that good may come? Whose condemnation is just"** (Rom.3:8). Clearly, using violence against abortion doctors and abortion clinics is not the Christian ethic.

Yes, I believe a preacher should leave politics out of the pulpit. You might ask why are you preaching on abortion. The answer is that first and foremost abortion is a moral and religious issue. Politicians may have abortion in the political arena, but that does not change the basic truth of the matter. We must remember that abortion is first and foremost an ethical question and only secondarily a political one. When politicians leave politics and go into the moral, ethical, and religious area, they have gone too far! When I preach on abortion, I am preaching on a moral, ethical, and religious issue that must be settled by the word of God—not by a political vote. Therefore, since abortion is a biblical issue, the answer to the problem must be settled by the Bible--not by the ignorant, unbiblical politicians.

We realize that 1 Peter 2:13 says, "Be subject to every ordinance of man for the Lord's sake," and Romans 13:1-7 teaches to obey civil government. But, what if civil government makes a law that violates God's law? Peter said in Acts 5:29, **"We must obey God rather than men."**

The Problem Today

On January 22, 1973 the Supreme Court of the United States gave a landmark decision in the Roe vs. Wade case. On that fatal day, a day which will live in infamy, the Supreme Court legalized abortion in every state. Before 1973, even the Supreme Court recognized that an unborn child was a human being. Does truth change? Human laws may change, but God's word does not change. On March 6, 1857, the Supreme Court ruled that Dred Scott, a black man, was not considered a person under the U.S. Constitution. If the Supreme Court made a terrible mistake in 1857, could they have made another one in 1973? Absolutely yes!

Did you know we have societies for the prevention of cruelty to animals and for the protection of unborn eagles, but we will grant no protection to unborn children? Did you know that teenage girls can go to abortion clinics in some states without their parent's consent, but these same children cannot have their ears pierced without written permission from a parent? I conclude that unborn eagles and piercing the ears are more important than an unborn child. Am I right? If not, why not? Several years ago a woman died in a car wreck—surgery was performed—the unborn child lived and inherited all her mother's possessions. Sometimes a pregnant woman is murdered, and her killer is charged with the murder of two human beings. The Court recognizes that the unborn child is a human being in this situation but denies personhood in abortion. Shame!

Some people today say that it is wrong to bring an unwanted baby into the world. I have one vital question—unwanted by whom? There are many childless couples who would love to have a baby. Many couples are on long waiting lists to adopt a newborn baby. Some people say that the woman, and the woman alone, has the right to determine whether or not to have the baby. I want to ask what choice does the unborn baby have. Some say that the unborn baby is not a child because it is dependent on the mother. That argument is absurd! Even after the child is born, it is still dependent on the mother or someone to take care of it.

The Basic Issue of Abortion

The most important question to be decided--is the unborn child a human being? Does the unborn child have a soul? Many think the unborn child is just a blob of tissue. Many look on aborting an unborn fetus like the removal of an abscessed tooth. Why do people believe this? Two reasons. First is because they believe that man is nothing more than flesh and blood and does not have an immortal soul. The second is they want the woman to have the final say.

Now, let us go back to the basic issue. Is the unborn child a human being? Does the unborn child have a soul? If the answer is yes, then those consenting to and partaking in wholesale abortion are committing murder. All killing is not murder, but murder involves killing. There are two types of killing that are not murder, capital punishment and self-defense (Ex. 22:2). My opinion is that abortion performed to save the life of the mother would not be murder. I realize there are sticky situations like rape and incest, but they are not the purview of this chapter.

What Early Christians Believed About Abortion

"Thou shalt not slay the child by procuring abortion; nor again, shalt thou destroy it after it is born" (*Epistle of Barnabas 19*—74 AD).

"You shall not procure an abortion, nor destroy a newborn child" (*Didache* 2:1—150 AD).

"There are some women among you who by drinking special potions extinguish the life of the future human in their very bowels, thus committing murder before they even give birth" (*Mark Felix, Octavius 30* – 170 AD).

"In our case, a murder being once for all forbidden, we may not destroy the fetus in the womb, while as yet the human being derives blood from the other parts of the body for its sustenance. To hinder a birth is merely a speedier man-killing; not does it matter whether you take away a life that is born, or destroy one that is coming to birth. That is a man which is going to be one; you have the fruit already in its seed" (*Tertullian, Apology 9:8*—210 AD).

"Now we allow that life begins with conception because we contend that the soul also begins from conception; life taking its commencement at the same moment and place that the soul does" (*Tertullian, Apology 27*—210 AD).

Many others equated abortion with murder, including Hippolytus (228 AD), Basil the Great (374 AD), John Chrysostom (391 AD), and Jerome (396 AD). From the beginning of early church history, abortion was considered a sin!

What the Bible Teaches About Abortion

In Genesis 25:21-22 Jacob and Esau are called "children" that "struggled within" Rebekah. Notice that even in the womb these boys are called "children."

In Exodus 21:22-25 Moses describes a case where a man strikes a pregnant woman, causing a premature birth. If there is no harm, the man is only fined. If harm ensues (i.e. the death of the baby), punishment is to be meted out proportionally. The guilty was to give "life for life." Please notice that the unborn fetus is just as much a human being as the mother in this passage. Unintentional life-taking was usually not a capital offense, but here it clearly was (Ex. 21:12-13).

In 2 Samuel 11:5 the unborn fetus is called a "child."

In Job 3:11-16 Job gives a list of people he would have been with if he died at birth. Included in the list are kings, counselors, princes, and those who had "a hidden untimely birth . . . as infants that never saw light" (i.e. stillborn or miscarried babies). Job is teaching that an unborn fetus is just as much a human being as a king or prince.

In Psalms 139:13-16 the unborn in the womb are formed by God. Notice the personal pronouns in the passage. God recognized David as a person before he was born.

In Proverbs 6:16-17 it is an "abomination" to God to shed innocent blood. The unborn are equal to live children. It is a sin to kill innocent children whether they are in the womb or out of it!

In Luke 1:36 the conceived unborn baby is called a "son."

In Luke 1:41-44 the unborn fetus is called a "babe" (Greek *brephos*). In Luke 18:15 and Acts 7:19, this same Greek word is used to describe young infants who had been born. In Luke 2:12 and 16 this Greek word *brephos* (babe) is used for Jesus after He was born. Therefore, we can conclude that a *brephos* is a human being whether in or out of the womb.

In my opinion, the strongest verse against abortion is James 2:26 which states, **"For as the body apart from the spirit is dead, even so faith apart from works is dead."** If the body without the spirit is dead, then the body with the spirit is alive. When the body is alive, the spirit is in the body. When the body is dead, the spirit leaves the body. When conception takes place in the womb, there is a body. True, it is microscopically small, but still there is a body. James 2:26 clearly teaches that if the unborn fetus is alive, then it has a spirit, a soul! In 1970, the California Medical Association stated, "Human life begins at conception." The International Conference on Abortion held at Washington, D.C. said, "Human life begins at the union of sperm and egg." Even the pro-abortionists admit that an unborn fetus is alive. The Bible teaches that an unborn child "leaps" and is "joyous." How can something that is not alive leap and be joyous? Ecclesiastes 11:5 states, "As thou knowest not what is the way of the wind, nor how the bones do grow in the womb of her that is with child." Obviously, dead things do not grow. Since the child is growing in the womb, it is alive and thus has a spirit, a soul! Wholesale abortion is murder—plain and simple! James 2:26 is powerful.

How Should Christians Respond to This Problem?

Christians must support and help the weak. Paul said we are to **"support the weak"** (1 Thess. 5:14). He also stated, **"Put on therefore, as God's elect, holy and beloved, a heart of compassion, kindness, lowliness, meekness, longsuffering"** (Col. 3:12). Who is more weak than the innocent unborn child? Who is more helpless than unborn babies unable to defend themselves? As Christians we cannot resort to violence and kill abortion doctors and bomb abortion clinics. That is unchristian and ungodly and sinful!

Paul wrote, "For though we walk in the flesh, we do not war according to the flesh (for the weapons of our warfare are not of the flesh, but mighty before God to the casting down of strongholds); casting down imaginations (i.e. reasoning's), and every high thing that is exalted against the knowledge of God" (2 Cor. 10:3-5). Elisha told his servant, **"Fear not; for they that are with us are more than they that are with them"** (2 Kings 6:16). Our weapons are **"mighty before God."** We must seek to lead others to a proper understanding of what God says about abortion. We must pray for our leaders (1 Tim. 2:1-4) and pray to God to intervene. We must vote for and elect those who respect God's word. We need to give financially to those who are fighting against abortion. We need to remember that sin is a reproach to any nation (Prov. 14:34). We should do whatever we can as peacemakers for the Lord to protect the helpless. We need to teach women who have had abortions that there is healing and forgiveness.

What About Women's Rights?

Many women will argue that they alone have the right to choose. They say they have the right to privacy and the right to control their own bodies. But, does a woman have the right to physically abuse her born children? If mothers cannot abuse a child after birth, then please tell me why they can abuse their child before birth? I want an answer to that question!

Many women say, "It's my own body." But, a pregnant woman is not one body but two. The woman's body is a host that nourishes the child. The child is a separate organism residing as a guest. To murder and abort a child in the name of private rights or personal choice or personal convenience is selfish and sinful. Many childless couples would love to adopt a newborn baby. Many couples would gladly pay the cost of the process.

Conclusion

We live in an ungodly world. In the name of personal choice and selfishness, millions of lives are being murdered every year. Isaiah said long ago, **"Woe unto them that call evil good, and good evil; that put darkness for light, and light for darkness; that put bitter for sweet, and sweet for bitter! Woe unto them that are wise in their own eyes, and prudent in their own sight!"** (Isa. 5:20-21). We are not to lean upon our own understanding but lean upon God's revealed word (Prov. 3:5; Matt. 4:4; Psa. 119:11, 105; 2 Tim. 3:16-17).

The moral confusion that exists today in America is caused by the deceitfulness of sin (Heb. 3:13) which darkens our understanding and alienates us from God and blinds us and makes us past feeling (Eph. 4:17-19). The only solution is to return to the moral compass of the word of God. Paul said, **"And now I commend you to God, and to the word of his grace, which is able to build you up, and to give you the inheritance among all them that are sanctified"** (Acts 20:32). If the word of God is not our guide, we are blind spiritually!

For Thought or Discussion

1 What is abortion?
2 How many abortions are performed in the world annually?

3 What is the major reason women give for an abortion?

4 Describe a person who refuses to hear both sides of an issue. Scripture?

5 Discuss Christians being involved in politics.

6 How should the issue of abortion be settled?

7 What happened on January 22, 1973?

8 Was the Supreme Court wrong on March 6, 1857? Why or why not?

9 If the Supreme Court was wrong in 1857, could they have been wrong in 1973?

10 (T or F) The unborn fetus is not a child because it is dependent on the mother.

11 Discuss: Is the unborn fetus a human being?

12 What did early Christians believe about abortion?

13 What does Exodus 21:22-25 teach?

14 What does Job 3:11-16 teach?

15 What is the significance of the Greek word *brephos?*

16 Use James 2:26 to show that abortion is murder.

17 How should Christians respond to the problem of abortion?

18 (T or F) A woman who has had an abortion cannot be forgiven.

19 (T or F) Christians should respond to abortion with violence.

20 What does Romans 3:8 teach?

21 Discuss a woman abusing her child after and before birth.

22 Discuss Isaiah 5:20 with the subject of abortion.

23 (T or F) Sin is deceitful. Scripture?

24 What is the only solution to abortion?

25 Discuss cases where abortion might be acceptable

Chapter 6-Speech

We are bombarded on all sides with foul language. Through the television, radio, movies, and videos, we constantly hear cuss words and terrible language. Candice Fuller, a Biology teacher at Garland High School, told me she was sick of hearing the F-word in her class. I taught math in public schools for forty-two years, and I will testify that the language used today by many students is atrocious!

Jesus said, **"And I say unto you, that every idle word that men shall speak, they shall give account thereof in the day of judgment. For by thy words thou shalt be justified, and by thy words thou shalt be condemned"** (Matt. 12:36-37). Zodhiates says "idle word" means "insincere language of a person who speaks one thing and means another." *Arndt-Gingrich* defines the Greek word *argos* as "a careless word which, because of its worthlessness, had better been left unspoken." This verse should grab our attention. Christians must be very careful with their speech. We will have to answer to the Lord on the day of judgment for our speech! When we are careless with our speech, we are being careless with our souls. Some Christians cuss and use bad speech and say, "Excuse my French." But, just saying "excuse it" does not excuse it with God. God will hold everyone accountable for his bad language.

We Must Have Sound and Honest Speech

The apostle Paul said we are to have **"sound speech, that cannot be condemned; that he that is of the contrary part may be ashamed, having no evil thing to say of us"** (Titus 2:8). He also said we are to use "wholesome words" (1 Tim. 6:3). Again he said, **"Let your speech be always with grace, seasoned with salt, that ye may know how ye ought to answer each one"** (Col. 4:6). Again, "Wherefore, putting away falsehood, speak ye truth each one with his neighbor: for we are members one to another" (Eph. 4:25). Again, **"Let no corrupt speech proceed out of your mouth, but such as is good for edifying as the need may be, that it may give grace to them that hear"** (Eph. 4:29). Again, **"Put away . . . shameful speaking out of your mouth. Lie not one to another; seeing ye have put off the old man with his doings"** (Col. 3:8-9). Again, "Take thought for things honest in the sight of all men" (Rom. 12:17). Peter wrote, "Having your behavior seemly among the Gentiles; that, wherein they speak against you as evil-doers, they may by your good works, which they behold, glorify God in the day of visitation" (1 Pet. 2:12). James said, "Out of the same mouth cometh forth blessing and cursing. My brethren, these things ought not so to be" (James 3:10).

A Strange Compliment

In the fall of 1972, I was finishing up my Bachelor's degree at Abilene Christian College. I was also working part-time at Gooch's Meat Packing Plant in Abilene. There were some unsavory people working there. Almost every word was a cuss word. However, my boss one time said to me, "John, I will give you fifty cents if you say a cuss word." I am not joking. He gave me one of the nicest compliments I have ever been given. This event proves that even though we may be around people who cuss and use foul language, we do not have to imitate their bad language.

The Ninth Commandment

The Ninth Commandment is **"Thou shalt not bear false witness against thy neighbor"** (Ex. 20:16). Some would suggest that this commandment was limited to false testimony in legal proceedings. This might be possible. But, Leviticus 19:11 states, **"Neither shall ye deal falsely, nor lie one to another."** Therefore, it appears to be far more likely that the word "bear" is used in its more normal usage relating to the regular affairs of daily life. The Hebrew verb "bear" (*'anah*) in the Old Testament literally meant "to answer or respond." It is found 316 times in the Old Testament. Only 22 times is it used in the restrictive sense of "testify" in a court of law. The ultimate purpose of the Ninth Commandment was to underscore the importance of the spoken word. The community had the right to expect truthfulness from each of its members. One's word was considered to be sacred. There is a responsibility not merely to avoid intentional falsehood, but also to be sure that accidental falsehood does not creep into our communication. That principle was true in Israel. It is also true in the Christian community, the Church. Jesus said, **"But let your speech be, Yea, yea; Nay, nay: and whatsoever is more than these is of the evil one"** (Matt. 5:37). Jesus upheld the validity of the Ninth Commandment in Matthew 19:18.

What Is a Lie?

Webster defines a lie as "a false statement or action, especially one made with the intent to deceive; anything that gives or is meant to give a false impression." Here are several other definitions: "an intentional misleading of another person; anything said or not said that deceives and misleads; anything that deceives or creates a false impression."

Abraham told Pharaoh (Gen. 12) and Abimelech (Gen. 20) that Sarah was his sister. This was a half-truth. A few Christians have told me that Abraham did not lie in either case. The overwhelming majority of scholars strongly disagree! Abraham may have been worried about his life, but his lie was going to cause adultery. Abraham concealed the truth that Sarah was his wife and thus he lied. Concealment of the truth becomes a lie when you have a moral obligation to the hearer. What Abraham told Pharaoh and Abimelech was deceitful (a lie) because they were using Abraham's information to do something sinful and evil (i.e. sleep with another man's wife). If concealment of the whole truth violates the second greatest commandment (Mark 12:31) and the Golden Rule (Matt. 7:12), the concealment is lying and sinful!

At a Christian college, a young Christian was majoring in missions. He was planning to spend his life in the mission field—somewhere in Africa. While he was in college, he started dating a young woman. They fell in love and got married. After the honeymoon, she told him that he'd better get his idea of going to Africa out of his head because she was not going. Certainly before the marriage, she knew that she did not want to be a missionary's wife. If she had been honest with him, which she wasn't, he never would have married her. One can be dishonest and deceitful by never saying a word— just like this woman.

In 1 Samuel 16:1-5 we have the story of how God told Samuel to conceal the truth from King Saul. This story proves that not all concealment is lying. Concealment becomes a lie only if what is kept from another is something he or she has the right to know for the sake of moral obligation. If concealment violates the second greatest commandment and the Golden Rule, then it is sin.

The Importance of Honesty

One's name, reputation, and integrity are built on honesty! Without honesty one has no character. Some people think that in order to get ahead in life, one must lie, cheat, and deceive. Today, many people believe that to shade a business deal, alter their IRS records, lie about selling a car, or cheat on a test is acceptable. The truthful person today is a rarity and a jewel. If one lies, his integrity is shattered, and it is next to impossible to put it back together. Once a person lies to you, how hard is it to believe him the next time? It has often been said, "Honesty is the best policy." How true!

Several years ago my grandfather had a verbal agreement with a friend about a business deal. When it came time to complete the transaction, his friend refused to keep his word. My grandfather said, "What hurts the worst is to realize I cannot depend on what he says. To lose faith in his honesty hurt worse than losing the deal."

Several years ago I received a phone call from a Church of Christ preacher. He asked me if I was interested in selling a product and making a little extra money. Since I was poor, I said, "Sure." I then asked him, "This is not Amway is it?" (Please note I have nothing against selling Amway.) He said it was (some company name that I do not remember). On a Saturday we met at the church building in the preacher's office to have some privacy. After about an hour of listening about the product line, he said it was Amway. I got extremely angry at him. I reminded him that I specifically asked him if the product was Amway. Although he did not say "no," he lied to me. He deceived me. I never would have met with him had he been upfront and honest. I told him if I wanted to sell Amway, I would contact my sister who sold it.

Honesty Should Always Be Given Lovingly

Paul said, **"Love . . . is kind"** (1 Cor. 13:4). In Ephesians 4:32 Paul said, **"Be ye kind one to another, tenderhearted."** He also said, "Put on therefore, as God's elect, holy and beloved, a heart of compassion, kindness, lowliness, meekness, longsuffering" (Col. 3:12). John wrote, "Beloved, let us love one another: for love is of God; and every one that loveth is begotten of

God, and knoweth God. He that loveth not knoweth not God; for God is love" (1 John 4:7-8).

Our honesty should always be given in a kind and loving manner! We do not have to be brutal in our honesty. Suppose a wife buys a dress. The husband does not have to say, "That is the ugliest dress I have ever seen." He could respond, "That is not my favorite. Your blue one is prettier."

When I was twenty-two years old, I asked my future wife if I was a good singer. (I wasn't and she knew it.) If she had said, "no"—that would have hurt my feelings. If she had said, "yes"—that would have been a lie. So she said, "You've got potential." She told the truth and told it lovingly. I guess on my tombstone they will put: "He had potential."

Liars Will Be Punished

In Deuteronomy 19:16-21 we find that honesty is a very serious subject with God. Notice that God calls false testimony "evil." Punishment would be rendered for false testimony—"life shall go for life, eye for eye, tooth for tooth, hand for hand, foot for foot."

In Proverbs 6:16-19 we learn that there are seven things which are an abomination to Jehovah. Notice that two of the seven are "a lying tongue" and "a false witness that uttereth lies." Proverbs 12:22 states, **"Lying lips are an abomination to Jehovah."** Proverbs 19:9 says, **"A false witness shall not be unpunished."** The Psalmist wrote, **"Thou wilt destroy them that speak lies"** (Psa.

5:6). In Acts 5:1-11 Ananias and Sapphira were struck dead because they lied.

Revelation 21:8 states, "But for the fearful, and unbelieving, and abominable, and murderers, and fornicators, and sorcerers, and idolaters, **and all liars, their part shall be in the lake that burneth with fire and brimstone; which is the second death."** Revelation 21:27 states, "And there shall in no wise enter into it anything unclean, or he that maketh an abomination and a lie: but only they that are written in the Lamb's book of life." Revelation 22:15 states, "Without are the dogs, and the sorcerers, and the fornicators, and the murderers, and the idolaters, and every one that loveth and maketh a lie."

Proverbs Teaches Us We Need Wisdom in Our Speech

Proverbs 15:2 states, **"The tongue of the wise uttereth knowledge aright; but the mouth of fools poureth out folly."** Proverbs 15:7 says, "The lips of the wise disperse knowledge; But the heart of the foolish doeth not so." There is no substitute for studying and knowing the word of God. This will enable us to disperse knowledge and truth. The word of God can build us up and take us to heaven (Matt. 4:4; Acts 20:32).

In Proverbs 27:5-6 we read, **"Better is open rebuke than love that is hidden. Faithful are the wounds of a friend."** Love prompts us to speak God's warnings to all who may be traveling toward spiritual destruction (Ezek. 33:8-9). Those who hear and heed will be forever grateful. If a friend wounds you by telling you something that is wrong in your life, he is truly a friend. Count yourself blessed if you have a friend like that. Open rebuke is better than love that is hidden.

Proverbs 18:7 states, "A fool's mouth is his destruction, And his lips are the snare of his soul." Proverbs 18:21 says, **"Death and life are in the power of the tongue."** Our words are powerful! Through our speech we can build up or destroy. Our words can be sharp as a sword (Prov. 12:18) and sharp as a razor (Psa. 52:2). One wife said, "I would rather my husband hit me physically, than to verbally abuse me in public." The Christian husband is to love his wife (Eph. 5:25). He should do neither.

Proverbs tells us, **"He that refraineth his lips doeth wisely"** (10:19) and **"He that spareth his words hath knowledge"** (17:27) and **"a fool uttereth all his mind"** (29:11). It is a mark of wisdom not to say everything that comes into our mind. We need wisdom to think about we say before we say it. This requires foresight and self-discipline. Proverbs 15:28 states, **"The heart of the righteous studieth to answer."**

Conclusion

It has been said there are three rules to follow when we speak. First: is it true? Second, is it kind? Third, is it needful? Would we want people to be honest with us? The Second Greatest Commandment and the Golden Rule teach us that we must be honest with others.

James says, "The tongue can no man tame, it is a restless evil, it is full of deadly poison" (James 3:8). The tongue cannot be tamed, but it can be controlled. The one who does control his tongue is "a perfect man"—that is, spiritually mature. We must strive to control our tongue every day of our lives.

For Thought or Discussion

1 Describe the speech of many today.
2 What did Jesus teach in Matthew 12:36-37?
3 Define the Greek word *argos* translated "idle word."
4 (T or F) Saying "Excuse my French" excuses bad language.
5 What kind of speech are Christians to have? (Titus 2:8)
6 What did Paul say in Eph. 4:29 and Col. 3:8?
7 What will cause non-Christians to glorify God? (1 Pet. 2:12)
8 What do you think about the compliment given to the author John Hobbs?
9 What was the Ninth Commandment out of the Ten?
10 (T or F) The Ninth Commandment was limited to the law courts.
11 (T or F) We should guard against unintentional falsehood.
12 What did Jesus mean in Matthew 5:37?
13 What is a lie?
14 Did Abraham lie when he said Sarah was his sister? Why or why not?
15 When is concealment a lie?

16   Why did God not sin in 1 Samuel 16:1-5?
17   What do you think about the preacher selling Amway? Did he lie?
18   How should honesty always be given?
19   What will happen to liars? Scriptures?
20   Compare the wise man and the foolish man by their speech.
21   What is better than love that is hidden? Scripture? Why?
22   What is the importance of Proverbs 18:21?
23   (T or F) It is a mark of wisdom to study and think before we speak.
24   Describe the tongue from James 3

Chapter 7-Gambling

A Christian could study the Bible from Genesis to Revelation, and he would never find the command "Thou shalt not gamble." Because of this truth some have concluded that gambling is not sinful. However, we need to remember that in Galatians 5: 19-21 Paul gives a list of sins that will cause a person to "not inherit the kingdom of God." Notice he includes the phrase "and such like." The point is that every sin is not specifically listed. Just because gambling is never specifically listed as a sin does not mean that it is not a sin! In 2 Timothy 3:16-17 we learn that Scripture gives us everything we need to be "complete, furnished completely unto every good work." Whether gambling is right or wrong will have to be determined by a serious study of Scripture! The word of God is our guide book to heaven (Acts 20:32; Matt. 4:4; John 12:48; Rev. 20:12).

What Is Gambling?

Gambling is defined by Webster as "to play games of chance for money or other stake; to take a risk in order to gain some advantage." Wikipedia states, "The wagering of money or something of material value on an event with an uncertain outcome with the primary intent of winning." It must be noted that gambling involves a creation of **unnecessary** risks which may endanger financial security.

Gambling is a moral/ethical issue confronting Christians. The government has sanctioned gambling by offering state lotteries and has provided easy access to lottery tickets in convenience stores. Gambling devastates families, destroys society, and decimates souls. It is easy to underestimate the deteriorating effects of gambling on our culture. Sadly, some religious groups encourage gambling. Dwayne Carpenter wrote, "Both the Catholic and Jewish traditions traditionally set aside days for gambling." If the states and some religious groups approve of gambling, what could possibly be wrong with it?

Arguments Used To Justify Gambling

Some will say that life itself is a gamble. They say "Well, everything in life involves chance." But, we are not talking about unnecessary risks. We understand that there is some chance in life. Solomon wrote, "I returned, and saw under the sun, that the race is not to the swift, nor the battle to the strong, neither yet bread to the wise, nor riches to men of understanding, nor yet favor to men of skill; but time and chance happeneth to them all" (Eccl. 9:11). The key phrase is "under the sun" which means "from a purely worldly perspective; without God's approval." Time and chance sometimes enables the swift not to win, the strong don't win the battle, and skilled men don't receive favor. God's will in our lives precludes a life of pure chance (1 Cor. 4:19; Jam. 4:15). We are to live to the will of God (1 Pet. 4:2). Life is not gambling; it involves seeking the will of God.

Some try to say that farming is a gamble. But, the farmer does not gamble in any wicked sense when he buys his seed and land, plants his crops, keeps the weeds out, and prepares for a bountiful harvest. His is a calculated risk, and not an unnecessary one, in order to ensure a harvest. His risks are based on the principle of sowing and reaping (Gen. 1:11; 1 Cor. 3:9; Gal. 6:7). Farming is an honorable way of receiving God's blessings (Psa. 104:14). Jesus did not condemn the farmer for his sowing of the seed (Mark 4:26-29). Farming is not gambling; it involves the activity of God.

Some say that buying insurance is a gamble. Again, it is a calculated risk, not an unnecessary one. By law you must have car insurance. The car insurance company does not want you to have a wreck. You do not want to have a wreck. But, if you do have a wreck, there is comfort knowing that you will be covered. On the other hand, there is the sad reality your insurance premiums will probably go up. Insurance is also a way of providing for one's family which is an important duty (1 Tim. 5:8). Insurance does not create the risk; but it is bought in order to protect one from times of illness, injuries, loss, or death. It is a wise investment. Those who obey the gospel, in a sense, are buying fire insurance—protection from eternal hell, if we are obedient to God's will (Rev. 2:10; 1 John 1:7).

Some say that investing in stocks and bonds is a form of gambling. It can be when speculative and significant risks are involved. But, buying and selling in order to get gain is not wrong. Jesus commended the five-talent and two-talent men because they invested their money (Matt. 25:14-30). In James 4:13-15 the writer does not condemn one for desiring to go into a city to buy and sell and get gain. James does condemn the attitude of leaving God out of his life and not recognizing that he has no lease on life. Receiving payment for allowing someone else to use one's money is not wrong.

Some say that gambling is not wrong if it is going for a good cause. But, the end never justifies the means (Rom. 3:8). If it is a good cause, people ought to support it because it is right. As a school teacher for forty-two years, I have had many students come to me wanting me to buy a raffle ticket for some organization. If my name is drawn, I would win a nice prize. Usually, I have just donated a dollar to their cause and denied myself the raffle ticket. In my opinion, the raffle draw is a form of gambling even though the amount of money is small and it is for a good cause.

Scripture Teaches That Gambling Is Sinful

The principle of gambling is sinful. Gambling violates the Christian work ethic. Paul wrote, **"Let him that stole steal no more: but rather let him labor, working with his hands the thing that is good, that he may have whereof to give to him that hath need"** (Eph. 4:28; cf. 1 Thess. 4:11-12; 2 Thess. 3:10-12). The Christian work ethic is to work, not gamble, to help others in need. Gambling may or may not enable one to help others. Working will always enable one to help others in need. Our gain is supposed to come from honorable labor, not from get-rich-quick schemes.

Gambling violates the stewardship ethic. God's word states, "For all things come of thee, and of thine own have we given thee" (1 Chron. 29:14). Peter said we are to be "good stewards of the manifold grace of God (1 Pet. 4:10). Paul states, "Here, moreover, it is required in stewards, that a man be found faithful" (1 Cor. 4:2). If we gamble with what God has given us, we are not good stewards. We will have to give an account for our stewardship. Do we want to give God a little of what we have or gamble it away and give Him nothing? A modern parable is "a bird in the hand is worth two in the bush." David said, **"Neither will I offer burnt-offerings unto Jehovah which cost me nothing"** (2 Sam. 24:24). To give God that which costs us nothing (like money won gambling) is an abomination.

Gambling is a greedy desire to gain money without work. Paul wrote, **"But they that minded to be rich fall into a temptation and a snare and many foolish and hurtful lusts, such as drown men in destruction and perdition. For the love of money is a root of all kinds of evil: which some reaching after have been led astray from the faith, and have pierced themselves through with many sorrows"** (1 Tim. 6:9-10). Greed traps the soul in covetousness and destroys the man from the inside. This greed and love for money leads to loss of faith and many sorrows. Proverbs 28:22 states, **"A man with an evil eye hastens after riches, and does not consider that poverty will come upon him."** Poverty is certainly implied in "many sorrows." Gambling seduces one with the opportunity to get rich quick without work. Study the life of Solomon. He was one of the richest men that ever lived. But, his riches did not solve his problems. It is the love of money that is sin—not having money. It is possible for one to have money and not love it and also possible not to have money and love money. It is the condition of our heart that determines our attitude and approach towards money.

Gambling encourages covetousness. Covetousness is "an inordinate desire for gain." A covetous man will not inherit the kingdom of God (Eph. 5:5) and will receive "the wrath of God" (Col. 3:6). Paul said that covetousness "is idolatry" (Col. 3:5). An idol is "anything that takes the place of God; excessive devotion to or reverence for some person or thing." Gambling cause's people to want something more than God, making it idolatry. Jesus warned us, **"Take heed, and keep yourselves from all covetousness: for a man's life consisteth not in the abundance of the things which he possesseth"** (Luke 12:15). Jesus then proceeds to give the parable of "a certain rich man" who was covetous. He was selfish and self-centered and never took God into account. Luke 12:20-21 states, **"But God said unto him, Thou foolish one, this night is thy soul required of thee; and the things which thou hast prepared, whose shall they be? So is he that layeth up treasure for himself, and is not rich toward God."** People gamble because they want to be rich, a desire we should flee (1 Tim. 6:9-11).

Gambling encourages laziness. If one gambles and wins a big pot one time, he thinks he can do it again. However, the law of probability is definitely against him winning again. Proverbs 21:25-26 NKJV states, **"The desire of the lazy man kills him, for his hands refuse to labor. He covets greedily all day long."** Solomon here is connecting greed and laziness. Gambling promotes a greedy desire to gain money quickly without work which leads to laziness.

Gambling leads to unsavory companions. Paul said, **"Be not deceived: Evil companionships corrupt good morals"** (1 Cor. 15:33). If a Christian has close friends who are motivated by greed and covetousness, they will influence him in an ungodly way. Proverbs

27:17 says, **"Iron sharpeneth iron; So a man sharpeneth the countenance of his friend."** When a knife is sharpened against iron, the interaction influences both instruments. So does friend influence friend. It's inevitable. The influence is so powerful that even the strongest cannot fail to absorb some of the ideals, disposition, morals, and language. We influence all we touch. All we touch influences us. Proverbs 13:20 states, **"Walk with wise men, and thou shalt be wise; but the companion of fools will be destroyed."** If our closest friends are fools and greedy people, we will suffer the consequences!

Gambling leads to addiction (cf. 2 Pet. 2:19). Gambling can become psychologically and physically addictive. Hans Breiter, MD wrote, "Monetary reward in a gambling-like experiment produces brain activation very similar to that observed in a cocaine addict receiving an infusion of cocaine." Have you ever heard of Gamblers Anonymous? The only requirement for membership is a desire to stop gambling. Their literature states, "Most of us feel that a belief in a Power greater than ourselves is necessary in order for us to sustain a desire to refrain from gambling." Sadly, many gamblers never conquer their addiction, and they pursue gambling into the gates of prison, insanity, or death.

Gambling is sinful because of the fruit it produces—greed, covetousness, laziness, poverty, divorce, neglected children, evil companions, failure to follow the Christian work ethic, etc. Jesus taught, **"Even so every good tree bringeth forth evil fruit; but the corrupt tree bringeth forth evil fruit. A good tree**

cannot bring forth evil fruit, neither can a corrupt tree bring forth good fruit" (Matt. 7:17-18).

The Results of Gambling

According to Gamblers Anonymous, there are at least 12 million compulsive gamblers in the United States right now. According to the *Dallas Morning News,* the average compulsive gambler has debts exceeding $80,000. This figure does not even come close to the social costs that result due to family neglect, embezzlement, theft, and involvement in organized crime. Sadly, people who gamble do not think or consider how they hurt themselves and others until it is too late.

The people that are affected the most from gambling are the poor and the disadvantaged. A New York lottery agent stated, "Seventy percent of those who buy lottery tickets are poor, black, or Hispanic." The National Bureau of Economic Research "shows that the poor bet a much larger share of their income." A major study on the effect of the California lottery came to the same conclusions. Those who are poor are more tempted to try and win it big so they can get out of their poverty. Sadly, all they do is dig themselves deeper and deeper into a hole.

Many suicides have occurred as a result of gambling. Many marriages have ended in a divorce and children being neglected all because of gambling. Another negative aspect of gambling is that the crime rate increases where there is gambling. In 1996, according to the *U.S. News and World Report,* "Crime rates in casino communities are 84% higher than the national average." There is a marked increase in welfare recipients with gambling problems; a rise in the number of bankruptcies; and an increased need for state-funded counseling centers for out-of-control gamblers.

Conclusion

After an examination of gambling, I am convinced that every honest truth-seeking Christian will understand that gambling is sinful. If we are wise, we will avoid it and teach the dangers and pitfalls of it. In addition to the toll it takes on the soul, gambling extracts a toll on society. Christians cannot engage in gambling of any kind and be acceptable to God. It does not matter what form of gambling is used or the amount of the wager, God is not pleased with those who gamble. If we are following the life of Jesus (1 Pet. 2:21; 1 John 2:6), we will not gamble. If we are trying our best to live a godly life (Matt. 5:48; Eph. 5:1; 1 Pet. 2:16-17), we will not gamble.

For Thought or Discussion

1 What verse in the Bible says, "Thou shalt not gamble?"
2 What is the point of the phrase "and such like" in Galatians 5:19-21?
3 What is our guide on this earth? Scripture?
4 Define gambling.
5 (T or F) Gambling involves unnecessary risks.
6 What precludes a life of pure chance?
7 Discuss why farming is not gambling.
8 (T or F) Insurance is a way of providing for one's family.

9 Why is investment in stocks and bonds not wrong?
10 (T or F) The end justifies the means. Scripture?
11 What is the Christian work ethic?
12 What was David's attitude about giving to God? Scripture?
13 (T or F) Money is a root of all kinds of evil.
14 What is the end result of the love of money?
15 What happens to the one with a greedy eye? (Prov. 28:22)
16 (Tor F) It is possible not to have money and yet love money.
17 What is covetousness? Scripture?
18 What is idolatry?
19 What did the Lord call the rich man in Luke 12:20-21? Why?
20 What does Proverbs 21:25-26 teach?
21 What happens to one who is the companion of fools?
22 What did Dr. Hans Breiter say about gambling?
23 (T or F) Gambling is sinful because of the fruit it produces.
24 Who is affected the most from gambling? Why?
25 What are some serious problems that come from gambling?

Chapter 8-Social Drinking

In discussion of Christian ethics, it becomes imperative that we discuss the topic of drinking. As we examine magazines and commercials on the television, we are bombarded with advertisements for alcoholic beverages. The problem of alcoholic consumption is somewhat unique in the discussion for Christian behavior. Most ethical questions are at least tentatively agreed upon by Christians as right or wrong. But, when it comes to drinking, many contend that "social drinking" is permissible. Some Christians think that to drink socially will help with business contacts. But, to be right with God is more important than a business contact (Mark 12:30). If a person gains the whole world but loses his own soul, what has he really gained (Matt. 16:26)?

The Danger of Alcoholic Consumption

A serious moral/ethical issue confronting Christians today involves the drinking of alcoholic beverages. Bridget Gant said, "More than 30% of Americans at some time in their lives has had an alcohol use disorder." Dr. James Garbutt said, "Nearly 100,000 people in America die every year of alcohol-related causes." It is the third leading cause of preventable mortality in the United States. Someone in our country is killed by a drunk driver every twenty-four minutes. Alcohol is typically found in the offender, victim, or both in about half of all homicides and serious assaults. Alcohol kills 2.8 million people every year globally. Alcohol causes cancer, heart disease, and liver disease. Many contend that alcohol is more dangerous than some illegal drugs like marijuana or ecstasy and should be classified as such. Alcohol is blamed for more than half of all visits to hospital emergency rooms.

Alcohol in the Book of Proverbs

Wine makes one not wise. Proverbs 20:1 states, **"Wine is a mocker, strong drink a brawler; and whosoever erreth thereby is not wise."** These are serious words that we must take to heart. If we want to be characterized by wisdom, we will stay away from wine!

Alcohol leads to poverty. Proverbs 21:17 says, **"He that loveth wine and oil shall not be rich."** Proverbs 23:20-21 reads, **"Be not among winebibbers, among gluttonous eaters of flesh: For the drunkard and the glutton shall come to poverty."**

Alcohol destroys lives. Read Proverbs 23:29-35 very carefully. Drinking brings woe, sorrow, contentions, complaining, and wounds without cause. The liquor "biteth like a serpent and stingeth like an adder." God points out in this text, (1) a vivid description of the effects of intoxicating drink, (2) a clear admonition to abstain and avoid it, and (3) a warning of what will happen if His warning is ignored.

Alcohol impairs judgment. Read Proverbs 31:1-5. These are the words of King Lemuel which his mother taught him. She instructs her son by saying, **"It is not** for kings to drink wine; nor for princes to say, where is strong drink? Lest they drink, and forget the law, and pervert the justice due to any that is afflicted." Every police officer will tell you that alcohol impairs judgment.

The Sin of Drunkenness

Drunkenness is strongly condemned in God's word. Paul wrote, **"Let us walk honestly, as in the day, not in rioting and drunkenness"** (Rom. 13:13). Paul also said, **"Or know ye not that the unrighteous shall not inherit the kingdom of God? Be not deceived: neither. . . drunkards . . . shall inherit the kingdom of God"** (1 Cor. 6:9-10). Again Paul said, **"Now the works of the flesh are manifest, which are these: . . . drunkenness . . . of which I forewarn you, that they who practice such things shall not inherit the kingdom of God"** (Gal. 5:19-21). God's word is clear. Unrepentant drunkards will not go to heaven. All of the sweet-sounding, eloquent words a preacher may use at a funeral service can never change the eternal fate of the drunkard.

Peter tells Christians **"be sober"** in 1 Peter 1:13. The words "be sober" come from the Greek *nephontes* which is from *nepho* which means "to be sober; not intoxicated; be self-controlled; **abstain from wine**; to be free from the influence of intoxicants." Again in 1 Peter 4:7 and 1 Peter 5:8 we have the instruction **"be sober."** Considering the Greek word *nepho,* these verses all teach us "to abstain from wine." The calls by God to "be sober" demand that we keep all of our senses sharp to use wisdom and discretion. Since alcohol hinders our judgment, diminishes our powers of reason, and dulls our awareness, it should be off limits to the Christian.

Did Jesus Endorse Social Drinking?

Invariably, those seeking to justify social drinking use John 2 as their favorite proof-text. Jesus was at a wedding in Cana (a social gathering). They ran out of wine and Jesus turned six pots of water (120-160 gallons) into wine. The problem deals with the word "wine." The Greek word is *oinos* which simply means "the juice of the grape." There is no way to go to the Greek text and determine whether the wine was fermented or unfermented. Fermented wine was to be avoided (Gen. 9:20-21; Prov. 23:29ff; Isa. 28:7). Unfermented wine was acceptable (Isa. 16:10; Jer. 40:10). Only the context can determine which "wine" (fermented or unfermented) was being discussed. The crux of the question is, "Did Jesus give intoxicating drink (fermented grape juice) to the crowd?" In light of Proverbs 20:1, **"Wine is a mocker, strong drink a brawler; and whosoever erreth thereby is not wise,"** it is inconceivable to teach that He gave intoxicating liquor. Also consider Proverbs 23:29-35; 31:1-5.

Habakkuk 2:15 says, **"Woe unto him that giveth his neighbor drink, to thee that addest thy venom, and makest him drunken also, that thou mayest look on their nakedness!"** This verse teaches it was a sin to give wine (fermented) to one's neighbor. Yet, Jesus never sinned (Heb. 4:15; 2 Cor. 5:21; 1 Pet. 2:22; 1 John 3:5). Therefore, Jesus could not have provided alcoholic wine to those at the wedding feast. To assert that He did is blasphemy and heresy of the highest degree! I have no problem believing that Jesus made a superior unfermented wine compared to anything that "the ruler of the feast" provided.

What About Social Drinking?

In spite of all the warnings in the Bible, many Christians think they can drink alcoholic beverages as long as they don't get drunk. Therefore, they say one can drink "socially" with no harm done. But, is one showing wisdom by drinking? Proverbs 20:1 teaches absolutely not! The Greek word *nepho* teaches absolutely not! Also, a weak brother may see you drinking and think it is permissible for him to drink. But, what if he cannot control his desire to drink? The strong Christian has contributed to the weaker brother's sin. Read Romans 14:13-15:3. Romans 14:21 says, **"It is good not to eat flesh, not to drink wine, nor to do anything whereby thy brother stumbleth."** Romans 15:1 says, "Now we that are strong ought to bear the infirmities of the weak, and not to please ourselves." In 1 Cor. 8:12 Paul wrote, **"And thus, sinning against the brethren, and wounding their conscience when it is weak, ye sin against Christ."** We must be willing to give up our rights so that we do not become a stumbling block to others. We do not want to influence others to partake of this evil and its disastrous effects. One time an elder drank alcohol at a social gathering. He did not realize that a member of the church was there and saw him. His social drinking gave him and the church a black eye.

Let us observe the statements of Peter: **"For the time past may suffice to have wrought the desire of the Gentiles, and to have walked in lasciviousness,**

lusts, winebibbing's, revellings, carousings, and
abominable idolatries" (1 Pet. 4:3). Notice that Peter
discussed the sin of "winebibbings" which is translated
"excess of wine" in the KJV. The Greek word means
"drunkenness." The word "carousings" is from the
Greek word *potois* which is translated "drinking parties"
in the NASV. I believe that Peter is showing that not
only is drunkenness sinful, but also that drinking parties
are sinful. What about those Christians who engage in
social drinking? Peter says the Christian **"no longer
should live the rest of your time in the flesh to the
lusts of men, but to the will of God"** (1 Pet. 4:2).
Social drinking of alcohol is living "in the flesh to the
lust of men." Christians have no business engaging in
social drinking. Christians should avoid and abstain from
this practice that destroys others as well as themselves.

Several years ago, a preacher was invited to speak
at an Alcoholics Anonymous meeting. At the end of the
program, the preacher was allowed to ask questions of
the hundred or more in the audience. This was the
question he asked to the alcoholics: "How did you get
started with alcohol?" The resounding answer was
"through social drinking." Paul said, **"Abstain from
every form of evil"** (1 Thess. 5:22).

When Is It Appropriate to Drink?

The rule for Christians is to abstain from alcohol.
We live by rules not the exceptions. The rules are what
we follow the majority of the time. However, I do
believe there are cases where it would be appropriate to
drink alcohol.

The apostle Paul told Timothy, **"Be no longer a drinker of water, but use a little wine for thy stomach's sake and thine often infirmities"** (1 Tim. 5:23). This passage does not authorize social drinking. Since Timothy was partaking of unfermented wine on the first day of every week in the Lord's Supper, the wine Paul is talking about is fermented wine. First, notice he said "use a little wine." Please circle the word "little." Secondly, notice he gives the reason to drink wine—"for thy stomach's sake and thine often infirmities." The passage is clearly discussing the use of wine in a medicinal capacity. When my wife and I had our first child Carlton, she breast-fed him (and our other three sons as well). Carlton absolutely refused to take a bottle. One time I tried to give him a bottle of breast milk, and you would have thought I was killing the kid. He would have nothing to do with it! When Mary Etta was breast-feeding Carlton, she developed plugged ducts in her breasts. As a result, she was unable to feed Carlton. Carlton was not going to take a bottle. This was definitely a major problem. Our doctor told her to drink a little wine (i.e. fermented wine) to clear up the problem. She did and it worked. Yea! She was able to nurse our son. Our son Carlton lived! Yea!

Proverbs 31:6 states, **"Give strong drink unto him that is ready to perish, and wine unto the bitter in soul."** This verse teaches to give strong drink (i.e. fermented alcohol) to one who is on his death bed to cut the pain. There is nothing wrong giving drugs to someone who is dying to lessen the pain. When I had knee surgery in college, I begged for the drugs to deaden the pain. I don't think I did anything wrong. I have never repented for asking for the drugs. Since then I have only taken powerful drugs in connection with surgery.

When you are in a foreign country and you do not have access to clean water, it is permissible to drink fermented wine. In Mexico if you drink the water, you will get "Montezuma's revenge." In India if you drink the water, you will get "Delhi belly." In 2004, I held a gospel meeting in Mexico. I was very careful not to drink the water. But, I did eat the food furnished by the Mexican brethren cooked in their water. When I got home, I was sick for three long days! That was a trip I will remember as long as I live.

When you are on the ocean and the ship is sinking, and there are not enough lifeboats, and the water is freezing, you can drink alcohol. On April 15, 1912, the Titanic sank in the Atlantic Ocean. One person was rescued which should capture our attention: the baker. He was one of the very few who was pulled from the freezing ocean. He had drunk a lot of alcohol. The alcohol in his veins enabled his blood not to freeze and thus he lived. Please notice that these examples are exceptions and not rules. We live by rules. The rule for faithful Christians is simply do not drink alcoholic beverages. It is not wise.

Conclusion

We need to ask "what is God's will regarding the consumption of alcohol?" In view of the warnings found in Proverbs: we want to be wise. Alcohol can lead to poverty, it can destroy lives, it impairs judgment—we should stay away from it. In view of the teaching found in the New Testament: we want to be sober, we are not to engage in drinking parties, we want to abstain from every form of evil, we need to be concerned regarding our influence on the weaker brother. In other words, we should stay away from it. One in three people who drink have succumbed to alcoholism. Social drinking has been a major cause of alcoholism. Do we really want to flirt with the seducing effects of alcohol? Alcohol can be tempting and easily ensnare the unsuspecting. One who drinks is playing with fire because every time he drinks there is the temptation to drink more. My Aunt LaFonne Hobbs wisely said, "No good can come from social drinking—only bad." I totally agree.

For Thought or Discussion

1　What makes the problem of social drinking unique?
2　How many people in America die every year from alcohol-related causes?
3　Discuss the dangers of alcohol.
4　From Proverbs 20:1 what makes one not wise?
5　(T or F) Alcohol leads to poverty.
6　How does Proverbs 23:29-35 describe drinking wine?
7　What does Proverbs 31:1-5 teach about wine?
8　(T or F) Unrepentant drunkards will go to an eternal hell of fire.
9　Define the Greek word *nepho*.
10　Why do some use John 2 as justification for social drinking?
11　What is the problem with the word "wine" in John 2?
12　What does Habakkuk 2:15 teach?
13　What does Romans 14:21 teach?

14 Discuss influencing the weaker brother.
15 What does 1 Peter 4:3 teach about drinking parties?
16 What has been a major factor in alcoholism?
17 (T or F) Christians should abstain from every form of evil.
18 (T or F) There may be times for a Christian to drink alcohol.
19 What does 1 Timothy 5:23 clearly teach?
20 (T or F) Mary Etta, my wife, did the right thing in seeking to save the life of our son.
21 What does Proverbs 31:6 teach?
22 What happens when you drink water in a foreign country?
23 What did the baker do on the Titanic in order to save his life?
24 (T or F) Alcohol can be tempting and easily ensnare one.
25 What are seven or eight reasons not to be involved with social drinking?

Chapter 9- Euthanasia

A moral/ethical issue that is increasingly confronting Christians today is euthanasia. The word "euthanasia" comes straight out of the Greek. The word *eu* means "good" and *thantos* means "death." Therefore, the word means "good death." Today, euthanasia commonly refers to a doctor inducing death with a legal injection, requested by a patient suffering terrible pain. Other names for this practice are "assisted suicide"; "aid in dying"; "death with dignity"; and "mercy killing." Some forms of voluntary active euthanasia are legal in the countries of Belgium, Luxembourg, The Netherlands, and Thailand. In the United States it is legal in Oregon and Washington. Passive euthanasia (i.e. pulling the plug) has long been accepted as legal. My father told me not to keep him alive by machines. What should Christians think concerning this issue?

The Foundation of the Problem

A world-wide ideological battle is raging which involves every person. There is no escape from it! Each person's view concerning euthanasia (and all other ethical issues) is determined by what he believes about man's origin, purpose, and destiny. There are basically two diverse philosophies, and it is not possible for anyone to embrace both. They are mutually exclusive. Do we believe in man (God's creation), the sanctity of life, belief in God, and preservation of life? Or do we believe that man is the product of evolutionary chance, the quality of life, playing God, and destroying life? We must go to the word of God to determine what is right and wrong! Scripture was given to us that we might be furnished unto every good work (2 Tim. 3:16-17).

What Is Man?

Genesis 1:26-27 states, **"And God said, Let us make man in our image, after our likeness. . . And God created man in his own image, in the image of God created he him; male and female created he them."** Genesis 2:7 says, "And Jehovah God formed man of the dust of the ground, and breathed into his nostrils the breath of life; and man became a living soul." One who understands that man is a dual being, created in His Maker's image, an immortal soul to live forever, knows the sacredness and preciousness of life. Since human life is sacred, then to willfully end it is wrong. This principle is firmly established in God's word. One thing the Lord hates is "hands that shed innocent blood" (Prov. 6:16-19). So it is a sacred duty to preserve and protect life to the glory of the One who gave it.

However, most of the leaders of the euthanasia movement deny the reality of a Supernatural Creator. This position forces any person to conclude that man is merely a product of evolutionary chance, an upright animal whose only destiny is a dusty grave and oblivion. One who accepts this premise would naturally have no conviction of the sanctity of life, and no hesitancy or remorse in ending human life. From this premise, euthanasia advocates claim they are acting in kindness by ending the life of any severely ill or suffering human being—just as one would shoot a sick horse! If man is nothing but a two-legged animal, then their reasoning is valid. If their reasoning is false (and we believe it is), their plans for society are among the most cruel, heartless, anti-God, anti-Christian ever conceived in the selfish minds of a perverted society. All who believe in God understand that man is not just an animal but a created being with an immortal soul. Dr. Matthew Connoly wrote, "Abandon God, and you, you can have euthanasia. Indeed, you will be hard put to escape it. But a good death it can never be! And no subterfuge of law like that before us today can ever make it so."

Human Life Is Sacred

Human life is sacred because God **"giveth to all life, and breath and all things . . . in him we live, and move, and have our being . . . for we are also his offspring"** (Acts 17:25-28). No human being ever has, or ever will have, power to create life. Nor does man have the power to decide whether he is mortal or immortal. Psalms 22:29 says, "None can keep alive his own soul." Only God has this power.

Genesis 9:6 states, **"Whoso sheddeth man's blood, by man shall his blood be shed: for in the image of God made he man."** Man's life is sacred for he is made in God's image. The one who sheds innocent blood becomes guilty and worthy of capital punishment. This principle is also taught in the New Testament. Paul taught that the civil government "beareth not the sword in vain" (Rom. 13:4). You kill people with a sword—you don't butter your bread with a sword. If the guilty are not punished, there is no way the innocent can be protected.

Yet it is very strange that those who oppose capital punishment for the guilty (even mass murderers) are usually in the forefront of the pro-abortion and pro-euthanasia campaigns to take the life of the innocent. God's word makes a clear distinction between life of the guilty and life of the innocent.

Our Bodies Belong to God!

Our bodies belong to God—not to us! This is especially true of Christians. Paul wrote, **"Or know ye not that your body is a temple of the Holy Spirit which is in you, which ye have from God? And ye are not your own; for ye were bought with a price: glorify God therefore in your body"** (1 Cor. 6:19-20). We no longer live for ourselves, but for God. Paul said, "For none of us liveth to himself, and none dieth unto himself. For whether we live, we live unto the Lord; or whether we die, we die unto the Lord: whether we live therefore, or die, we are the Lord's" (Rom. 14:7-8). Again Paul said, **"And he died for all, that they that live should no longer live unto themselves, but unto him who for their sakes died and rose again"** (2 Cor. 5:15). We might prefer death, but the Lord may have a different plan for us (Phil. 1:21-24).

Examples of Suicide in the Bible

Suicide, in general, is an act of murder which is sinful and immoral. God's word states very clearly, **"Thou shalt not murder"** (Exodus 20:13; Matt. 5:21). Every example of suicide in the Bible was by a sinful man. Abimelech asked his armor bearer to kill him, and he did as requested (Judges 9:50-54). Saul, who was gravely wounded, fell on his own sword (1 Sam. 31:3-4).

In 2 Samuel 1 we learn that Saul begged an Amalekite, "Stand beside me and slay me for anguish has seized me and yet my life still lingers." The Amalekite's response was exactly that of those who believe in euthanasia. He said, "So I stood beside him and slew him because I was sure that he could not live after he had fallen." David was incensed. David described the act as **"putting forth the hand to destroy."** David had the Amalekite killed for his assassination. Evidently David, a man after God's own heart (1 Sam. 13:14), did not agree with the concept of euthanasia. Ahithophel hanged himself (2 Sam. 17:23). Zimri burned himself alive (1 Kings 16:18-19). Judas hanged himself (Matt. 27:5). Faithful men of God chose to endure pain rather than end life by suicide (murder). Job suffered immensely but not for sins he committed (Job 2:7-10; 27:5-6). Job longed for death, but he refused to kill himself (Job 3:1-11; 6:8-9; 19:25-27; 23:10). Job's wife said, "Curse God and die." For those who practice euthanasia, this would have been the answer to Job's suffering. But, Job called this act "foolish." Jehovah Himself said Job was "a perfect and upright man, one that feareth God, and turneth away from evil" –Job 1:8. Jeremiah suffered with those who had sinned (Lam. 3:38-41). He was constantly in danger of losing his life (Jer. 26:8-24). But, he chose to be obedient to God even in the fear of death. The apostle Paul suffered tremendously for preaching the gospel (1 Cor. 4:9-13; 2 Cor. 11:23-28). But, he never chose suicide.

The Value of Suffering

The unbeliever scoffs at the Christian ethic which teaches there is value in suffering. But, God's word clearly teaches it! Paul said, **"For our light affliction which is for the moment worketh for us more and more exceedingly an eternal weight of glory"** (2 Cor. 4:17). Just think—our afflictions are working for our eternal glory. Wow! We will be rewarded in heaven for our steadfast obedience in tough times (Rev. 2:10; James 1:12). Again Paul said, "If we endure, we shall also reign with him" (2 Tim. 2:12). He also said, **"We also rejoice in our tribulations: knowing that tribulation worketh stedfastness"** (Rom. 5:3). James said we are to "count it all joy, my brethren, when we fall into manifold temptations" (Jam. 1:2). Why? Faithfulness in suffering produces maturity and patience. Peter wrote, **"That the proof (i.e. the trying and testing) of your faith, being more precious than gold that perisheth though it is proved by fire, may be found unto praise and glory and honor at the revelation of Jesus Christ"** (1 Pet. 1:7). Paul endured suffering to demonstrate the power of Christ in his life (2 Cor. 4:8-12). He also viewed affliction as an opportunity to provide an example for others (2 Cor. 1:3-11). One preacher said, "How we die may be our last opportunity to magnify the Lord and help others."

Honor the Elderly

The Fifth Commandment is: **"Honor thy father and thy mother"** (Ex. 20:12). Moses wrote, **"Remember the days of old, consider the years of many generations: ask thy father, and he will show** thee; thine elders, and they will tell thee" (Deut. 32:7). Again he wrote, "Thou shalt rise up before the hoary (i.e. white) head, and honor the face of the old man, and thou shalt fear thy God" (Lev. 19:32). Paul said, "But if any provide not for his own, and specially his own household, he hath denied the faith, and is worse than an unbeliever" (1 Tim. 5:8). It is inconceivable that anyone who truly honors his parents (or any other person) would resort to deliberate killing. Surely no reasonable person would conclude that "provide for his own household" means to leave a suicide pill beside the bed or provide a lethal injection of barbiturate! How tragic it would be to make one's parents feel guilty for living. It is inhuman to think of sacrificing the hoary head to fatten the purse of those left behind. Yet this is the theme laced throughout the current euthanasia propaganda.

Heed the Cry of the Elderly

Psalms 71:9 and 18 state, "Cast me not off in the time of old age; forsake me not when my strength faileth . . . Yea, even when I am old and gray headed, O God, forsake me not: until I have declared thy strength unto the next generation, thy might to everyone that is to come." Such was the cry of the Psalmist's heart, a plea which has echoed down through the ages even until now. Though the request is made to God, we understand that God works through His people. This places on us a special responsibility to see that this cry of the aged is heard and heeded. Read again the Scripture given above. Note the richness of its meaning. The reason the Psalmist wanted to live, even when he was old and grayheaded, was that he had a desire to show

God's strength and power to his generation and "to everyone that is to come." In other words, he had knowledge and experience and testimony concerning God which he knew to be valuable to others, including succeeding generations. So he prayed for continued life to share this even "when my strength faileth." Talk about productivity! There's absolutely no way to measure the value of such assets to society. How far above mere economic productivity! Yet, if those who favor euthanasia have their way, these precious treasures which reside in the elderly will be completely lost. It would be a sad day in the history of civilization for a people to trample these Scriptures into the dust and formulate a new philosophy devoid of compassion and care, one that has dollar signs written all over it, one that would kill the aged, the handicapped, the poor, the unwanted—and who knows which ones may be targeted next?

Euthanasia Is Packaged As a "Right"

Isn't it amazing and incredible that anything, it seems—even murder—can be sold to the public as long as it is labeled, packaged, and peddled as a "right"? Many are loudly saying "Suicide is your right—a viable option if life is too tough for you to handle." Death is one absolute certainty facing each person. Therefore, nothing is more personal or imperative than to know what the euthanasia advocates have in mind for you and your family. *The American Medical News* (5-17-85) admits: "A terrifying and hitherto unthinkable 'solution' to worldwide increases in health care costs is surfacing." Many say that euthanasia is one way to save families money. Plans have been made to push legislation in all fifty states. It is titled the "Uniform Rights of the

Terminally Ill Act." Dr. Robert Barry said, "Passage of the 'Uniform Rights of the Terminally Ill Act' will grant legal approval for suicide, assisted suicide and non-voluntary mercy-killing in some instances." Advocates emphasize two rights, the right to die and the right to kill. They view their work as a "human rights" movement, identifying the "right to self- determination in dying." They claim the when, where, how, and why to die as one of the most personal rights. Allan Pollack wrote, "Everyone has a right to end their own life—even a child. We can help them to consider and make the choice . . . but the choice still belongs to the person. If we do not allow children or the incompetent to commit suicide or have euthanasia administered, we are really practicing age discrimination and illness discrimination."

Who Advocates Euthanasia?

The movement in the U.S. dates back to 1938 when Charles F. Potter, signer of the Humanist Manifesto I in 1933, founded the Euthanasia Society of America. The name was later changed to the Society for the Right to Die. In 1954 Joseph Fletcher wrote *Morals and Medicine* in which he advocated voluntary euthanasia. He also endorsed abortion, death with dignity, and the right to suicide. Those who embrace reincarnation (e.g. the New Age Movement) would accept euthanasia as a gracious favor to aid a suffering soul to leave a pain-racked body and enter another body. Elizabeth Kubler-Ross believes in reincarnation. She says, "You have endless chances," stating that eventually "everyone will pass though it may literally take an eternity." Of course, this teaching is totally anti-biblical. Hebrews 9:27 states, **"And inasmuch as it is appointed unto men once to**

die, and after this cometh judgment." Paul taught in 2 Cor. 5:10 we are going to be judged by "the things done in the body"—not out of the body! We will not get a second chance after we die. You can readily see that anyone who believes in many lives and eventual "graduation" for everyone would feel little concern over either euthanasia or suicide, believing it could be one's "advancement."

Secular Arguments Against Euthanasia

If euthanasia were made legal, it would be virtually impossible to determine whether the motive of the killer came entirely from greed or other selfish reasons. Supposed terminal illnesses can be misdiagnosed so that patients may feel inclined to make needless requests for a merciful death. Even conditions thought to be terminal may undergo unexpected remission. The medical books are full of cases where near-death patients experienced remarkable recoveries. Mistakes can be made with regard to supposed "incurable" diseases. The disease may be incorrectly diagnosed or may be able to survive or be cured.

Conclusion

Voluntary active euthanasia (suicide), even when one is suffering, can be viewed as (1) an act of ingratitude toward God who gives us both life and suffering for our good, (2) a violation of our duty to serve God all the days of our lives, (3) a misguided effort to escape an aspect of life that God intends for us to experience, (4) a selfish act that hurts those closest to us, depriving them of our love, example, and influence, (5) and very simply—murder! The story of Saul's death and

David's response speaks volumes! We should not hasten our death just to avoid suffering. We can and should use our suffering to help and comfort others (2 Cor. 1:3-5). We do not know what the future holds. There could be a cure, remission, or answer to prayer right around the corner. There is nothing wrong with trying to alleviate the pain via pain killers (Prov. 31:6). But, we must not take a life! It is sinful to murder (Matt. 5:21). Our lives belong to God, and we must trust in Him. Paul wrote, **"There hath no temptation taken you but such as man can bear: but God is faithful, who will not suffer you to be tempted above that ye are able; but will with the temptation make also the way of escape, that ye may be able to endure it"** (1 Cor. 10:13).

For Thought or Discussion

1 Define euthanasia.
2 What are some other names for euthanasia?
3 What is passive euthanasia?
4 What is the ideological battle in the euthanasia debate?
5 (T or F) God hates one that sheds innocent blood. Scripture?
6 Describe man from Genesis 1-2.
7 What is the view of the leaders of the euthanasia movement?
8 Why is human life sacred?
9 Discuss capital punishment.
10 What is strange about those who oppose capital punishment?
11 What did Paul teach in 1 Corinthians 6:19-20?
12 In general, why is suicide considered murder?
13 What did Job say to his wife when she told him to

die?

14 How did faithful, godly men view suffering?

15 Why is there value in suffering?

16 What is "more precious than gold"? Why?

17 (T or F) Leaving a suicide pill by the bed shows honor for one's parents.

18 What is the cry of Psalms 71:9 and 18?

19 Discuss euthanasia as a right?

20 Why would the New Age Movement accept euthanasia?

21 What do Hebrews 9:27 and 2 Corinthians 5:10 clearly teach?

22 How can we view active euthanasia.

23 What did Paul teach in 2 Corinthians 1:3-5?

24 What did Paul teach in 1 Corinthians 10:13?

25 What are some secular arguments against euthanasia?

26 What did David do that shows he was opposed to euthanasia?

27 (T or F) David was a man after God's own heart. Scripture?

Chapter 10- Attendance

Christian ethics is following the life of Jesus. We are told to **"follow his steps"** (1 Pet. 2:21) and **"to walk even as he walked"** (1 John 2:6). Jesus went to Bible study **"as his custom was"** every week (Luke 4:16). He set the example for us to follow. And yet, some Christians do not understand they are living in sin by forsaking the assembly.

True Stories

I was the pulpit preacher at Hillcrest Church of Christ in Coleman, Texas, from November 1998 to May 2002. I had been there about two years when a lady and her young son came on a Wednesday night. I had never seen this woman. She was actually the daughter of a couple who attended Hillcrest. After the service was over, she came to the front and asked that her son be baptized. The preacher before me also attended there. He said he would do it. I found out that the woman lived in Coleman and could have attended all the time. Sadly, we never saw the woman or her son again. I am sure she left thinking "I am a good mother. I got my son baptized. I got my son saved. I am a good mother." However, the sad truth was she was a terrible mother! She did not set the right example by attending faithfully. She did not teach her son to love God (Mark 12:30; John 14:15) and to attend the services faithfully (Heb. 10:25). Sad!

I have performed my share of funerals. Many times I have been told that the one who died was baptized at a young age but had not attended services in forty years. That has caused the family to have false hope that somehow their loved one's eternal fate was all right. I have been given written statements by the family that they wanted read from the pulpit that basically taught that their unfaithful loved one is going to heaven. I have refused to read it. It made them mad and angry with me. But, I am not going to mislead. That would be a sin on my part.

Several years ago I read in the newspaper a statement by a woman. She was downplaying the need to attend church services faithfully. She wrote, "I just don't feel that heaven is open only to church-goers." There are so many things wrong with her quote. First, she was leaning upon her own understanding instead of God's revealed word (Prov. 3:5-6; 28:26; Isa. 5:20-21; John 12:48; Rev. 20:12). Second, she did not understand what God's word teaches about the importance of attendance. Third, she did not understand the importance of loving God and how one loves God.

One year the Dallas Cowboys were in the Super Bowl. One member told me he was not coming to church that Sunday night because he wanted to watch the Cowboys. He said if he came, his heart would be concerned with the game and not the church service. He showed where his heart was (Matt. 6:21). Sadly, his heart was not right before God (Acts 8:21). The Dallas Cowboys did not die for his sins! What do you think the Lord will say to him on the Day of Judgment?

Does One Who Forsakes the Assembly Love God?

Jesus said, **"And thou shalt love the Lord thy God with all thy heart, and with all thy soul, and with all thy mind, and with all thy strength"** (Mark 12:30). This is the first and greatest commandment. But the question comes—how do we love God? The answer is really quite simple. The Bible teaches very clearly the way we love God is to obey Him (John 14:15-24; 15:10-14; 1 John 2:3-6; 5:3; and 2 John 6). John wrote, **"He that saith, I know him, and keepeth not his commandments, is a liar, and the truth is not in him"** (1 John 2:4). If someone claims to love the Lord but does not keep His commandments, he is a liar! Hebrews 10:25 says, **"Not forsaking our own assembling together, as the custom of some is, but exhorting one another and so much the more, as ye see the day drawing night."** The word "forsaking" comes from *egkataleipontes* which means "forsake, abandon, desert, leave behind, neglect." When a Christian forsakes and neglects the assembling, he sins, and more importantly, he does not love God! One cannot love God and disobey him. That is impossible!

Some people have said to me, "John, when I am out on the lake fishing on Sunday morning, I feel so close to the Lord. I have an intimate personal worship service with the Lord. So, it cannot be wrong if I go fishing on Sunday." The problem with this action is very simple—it is not obeying the Lord. We are commanded to assemble with the saints. Not obeying the command to assemble is sinful!

Jesus Said, "This Do in Remembrance of Me"

When it comes to partaking the Lord's Supper, Jesus said, **"This do in remembrance of me"** (1 Cor. 11:24). However the question is "How often do we partake of the Lord's Supper?" Acts 20:7 states, **"And upon the first day of the week, when we were gathered together to break bread."** Paul said, **"For as often as ye eat this bread, and drink the cup, ye proclaim the Lord's death till he come"** (1 Cor. 11:26). The question is how often is "often"? When we read 1 Corinthians 16:1-2, we discover the church was coming together on **"the first day of every week."** Church history also reveals to us a weekly observance of the Lord's Supper. *The Teaching of the Twelve Apostles* (120 A.D.) states, "But every Lord's day do ye gather yourselves together and break bread." Augustus Neander says, "It was the practice of the early church to partake of the Lord's Supper every Sunday." *The International Standard Bible Encyclopedia* says, "In the post-apostolic church the Eucharist (i.e. Lord's Supper) continued to be celebrated every Lord's Day (i.e. Sunday)." Therefore, if one is out fishing or playing golf on Sunday, he is not doing what Jesus said to do! Jesus said, **"Why call ye me Lord, Lord and do not the things which I say?"** (Luke 6:46). We are either going to do what Jesus said to do, or we are not going to do what He said. If we don't, we are disobedient and sinful! If we don't, we do not love Him! Our love for the Lord will never rise higher than our obedience to His commands!

Are There Excuses/Reasons To Miss the Assembling?

Yes, I believe there are times we must miss the assembly. If our ox is in the ditch, we have to get the ox out. Certainly, God is a kind, loving, caring, and understanding God. The bottom line is simply this: whatever excuse/reason we give for missing the assembly, we better be prepared to give it to the Lord on the Day of Judgment because we will be called to do so! Every one of us needs to ask ourselves honestly: will my excuse be accepted by God? When I was a young child with chicken pox, my mother stayed home with me on Sunday morning while my dad went to church. On Sunday night, they reversed their roles. He stayed home while my mother went to church. Suppose a woman is having a baby. Her "ox is in the ditch" and obviously, she cannot attend the assembly. I am confident the Lord understands. If you are sick, you need to stay home. You do not want to go to the assembly and spread your germs all around. That is not loving your neighbor. When I have had surgery, I have had to miss.

Hebrews 10:25 Is Just As Important As Other Scriptures

Notice Hebrews 10:25 "**not** forsaking" with Romans 13:9 "thou shalt **not** commit adultery" and "thou shalt **not** murder" and "thou shalt **not** covet." There is no Scripture that teaches one of these **"not's"** is any greater sin in His eye than the other. Yet, there are brethren who shame the stealer with a "How could you?" and then forsake the assembly as if it were an optional thing. When Moses came down from Mount Sinai, he came down with Ten Commandments. He did not come down with Ten Suggestions. God gave instructions, and He wants His instructions obeyed. Eight of the Ten are negative! When God says don't do something, He means don't do it! One of the commandments we are given is: **"Not forsaking the assembling."** Paul wrote, **"Let no man deceive you with empty words: for because of these things cometh the wrath of God upon the sons of disobedience"** (Eph. 5:6). The Lord is going to render vengeance to those who do not continue to obey the gospel (2 Thess. 1:7-10). John 3:36 states, "He that obeyeth not the Son shall not see life, but the wrath of God abideth on him." Those who do not obey the truth shall receive "wrath and indignation, tribulation and anguish" (Rom. 2:5-9).

What Is "the Day Drawing Nigh" in Hebrews 10:25?

There are four main views: (1) Sunday, the first day of the week, (2) the second coming of Christ, (3) the destruction of Jerusalem, and (4) the day of assembling (whenever that day is). This is a good study, but the answer is not the salient point of this chapter. If we never did settle or agree on what day was under discussion in the text, it would never erase the plain command of Hebrews 10:25 **"not forsaking the assembling of yourselves together."** Instead of focusing on "the day," we need to focus on "the assembling." The assembling is not partaking of the Lord's Supper or giving as we have been prospered or praying. The "assembling" is the church coming together! It is the church coming together that we are not to forsake or neglect.

Let Us Discuss the Assembly

Some assemblies the Lord has called. We are to meet on the first day of every week to engage in the five acts of worship (singing, giving, praying, reading and studying God's word, the Lord's Supper). So, we have no option, no choice. We must meet and obey God. Some assemblies the elders have called. Brethren, it is simply wrong, false doctrine, and sinful to say that when elders call an assembly, it is optional. Elders are required to "feed the flock" (Acts 20:28). To do this they must set up specific feeding times for that feeding. Hebrews 13:17 states, **"Obey them that have the rule over you, and submit to them: for they watch in behalf of your souls, as they that shall give account; that they may do this with joy, and not with grief: for this were unprofitable for you."** Look carefully at this verse. God says, "Obey them" and "submit to them." Why? One reason is because God said to do it. A second is because elders will give account for our souls. A third is because if we don't, it is "unprofitable" for us. The word "unprofitable" is from the Greek *alusiteles* which means "unprofitable, harmful, hurtful, useless, detrimental, ruinous, and disastrous." If we do not obey and submit to the elders, it is harmful and detrimental to us. We are actually hurting ourselves which is unwise (Prov. 8:35-36).

Several years ago there was a cartoon that came out in a religious magazine. The cartoon had a long line of people waiting to be judged. All of a sudden there is a tremendous roar of approval at the front of the line. One guy in line taps the shoulder of the man in front of him and asks, "Why are people yelling with happiness?" The man turns around and says, "Wednesday nights don't count." Now brethren, that is a joke. If we can make it to services on Wednesday nights, the Lord expects us to go.

We Are To Be Zealous!

Jesus said, **"Seek ye first his kingdom, and his righteousness; and all these things shall be added unto you"** (Matt. 6:33). Are we truly seeking first His kingdom and His righteousness if we forsake the assembling? Paul said we are to be **"zealous of good works"** (Titus 2:14). The word "zealous" means "to have an intense desire." Do we have an intense desire to be obedient to the Lord? Jesus said, **"So because thou art lukewarm, and neither hot nor cold, I will spew thee out of my mouth"** (Rev. 3:16). Christians who are "lukewarm" in attending the assemblies are not zealous of good works and will be rejected by the Lord. When there is an empty seat at the building and that seat should be occupied by you, it is in effect saying to God, "When I don't need you, I will not be there." Do we really think that will hold water before the Lord? The bottom line is simply that Christians who do not attend like they should are not **"zealous of good works"** and do not love the Lord. Christ's love, demonstrated by dying on the cross for us, should motivate us to be faithful and obedient and to live for Him (2 Cor. 5:14-15).

The Context of Hebrews 10:25

Read carefully Hebrews 10:25-31. To forsake or neglect the assembly is willful sin. Examine the seven consequences of willful sin: (1) There is no more a sacrifice for sins. Jesus's death will not cover willful sin.

In the Old Testament there was no forgiveness for the high-handed sin (Numbers 15:28-31). (2) There is "a certain fearful expectation of judgment, and a fierceness of fire which shall devour the adversaries." (3) Those who set aside Moses' law died without mercy or compassion. But, those who willfully forsake the assembly under Christ's covenant are warned of a "sorer punishment." (4) Trodding underfoot the Son of God is connected with those who willfully forsake the assembling. (5) Counting the blood of the covenant, where we were sanctified, an unholy thing—i.e. take it or leave it; attend or not attend; it really does not make much difference—is connected with those who willfully forsake the assembly. (6) Doing despite unto the Holy Spirit of grace is connected with those who willfully forsake the assembling. (7) The vengeance of God and recompense of reward He pours out when He judges His people is a warning for those who would willfully forsake the assembly.

Why such strong and fire-charged language? God is telling us that willfully forsaking the assembly is a sin, and He will punish those who disobey! We must take this strong warning from God very seriously. 2 Peter 3:9 says that God is **"not wishing that any should perish, but that all should come to repentance."** Paul said that God **"would have all men to be saved, and come to the knowledge of the truth"** (1 Tim. 2:4).

Conclusion

One time a son had been away from home a long time. He called his mother and told her that he was coming home and looking forward to seeing her. When he arrived home on Sunday night, she was not there. Shortly after, she came walking in the door. Her son said, "Mother, where were you? I was hoping to see you as soon as I arrived. I called and told you I was coming." She replied, "Someone called before you did." Almost indignantly he said, "Who called that was more important than me?" To which she replied, "The Lord." The Lord is more important than anyone or anything. Jesus taught in Matthew 10:34-39 that we must love Him more than husband, wife, father, mother, son, or daughter. The question must be asked. Do we really love the Lord if we forsake and neglect the assembly? Are we truly following the example of Jesus when we neglect and forsake the assembly?

For Thought or Discussion

1 What verses teach that we are to follow the example and life of Jesus?
2 What was the custom of Jesus?
3 What do you think about the mother in Coleman?
4 (T or F) Baptism is a paid ticket to heaven.
5 (T or F) Some people act like baptism is a paid ticket to heaven.
6 Discuss: "I just don't feel that heaven is open only to church-goers."
7 What is the most important Commandment? Scripture?
8 How does one love God? Scriptures?
9 Define the word "forsaking."
10 Why can one not worship God acceptably on Sunday while fishing?
11 (T or F) One who forsakes the assembly violates 1 Cor. 11:24.

12 What NT verses teach that we are to observe the Lord's Supper every Sunday?

13 (T or F) Church history says the early church observed the Lord's Supper every Sunday.

14 What are some justifiable reasons to miss the assembly?

15 What is the bottom line on missing the assembly?

16 How many of the Ten Commandments are negative?

17 What happens to the disobedient? Scriptures?

18 What does Hebrews 13:17 teach? Why?

19 Define the word "unprofitable."

20 What are we to seek first in our lives? Scripture?

21 (T or F) One who forsakes the assembling is seeking the Lord first.

22 Discuss the difference between "zealous" and "lukewarm."

23 What are the seven consequences of willful sin?

24 Why does God use such strong language in Hebrews 10:25-31?

25 What did Jesus teach in Matthew 10:34-39?

Chapter 11- Immodest Apparel

A moral/ethical issue confronting Christians every day pertains to immodest apparel. Should Christian women wear shorts, miniskirts, low-cut blouses, tight skirts, or tight pants? Some women declare, "It's nobody's business what I put on my body." However, a Christian must have this attitude: "Would the Lord be pleased with my attire?" Jesus said, **"For I do always the things that are pleasing to him"** (John 8:29). Paul said, **"For Christ also pleased not himself"** (Rom. 15:3). The Lord owns our bodies (1 Cor. 6:19-20). Therefore, it becomes a principle of Christian ethics to determine what Christian women wear! Paul said, **"Whatsoever ye do, do all to the glory of God"** (1 Cor. 10:31).

It Is Shameful To Expose One's Nakedness

After Adam and Eve sinned, "They sewed fig-leaves together, and made themselves aprons" (Gen. 3:7). The word "aprons" has a marginal reading in the ASV as "girdles." The NKJV translates the Hebrew word as "coverings." The Hebrew word is *chagorah* which means "a garment covering the midsection." Even though Adam and Eve made a covering for themselves, they still felt naked (Gen. 3:10-11). Evidently, God was not pleased with the brevity of the "coverings" they had made. So, He made "coats of skins and clothed them" (Gen. 3:21). The word translated "coats" is the Hebrew word *kethoneth* which referred to "a garment commonly reaching to the knee."

Since each one in Christ, male or female, is a priest of God (1 Peter 2:5-10), it is wise to note that God called for a special dress for His priests in the Old Testament when they came to minister before Him and for Him. As they ministered, they were to have on special attire, including "linen breeches to cover the flesh of their nakedness; from the loins even unto the thighs they shall reach . . . Neither shalt thou go up by steps unto mine altar, that thy nakedness be not uncovered thereon" (Exodus 28:36-42; 20:26). In the Old Testament, exposure of private body parts was often a form of judgment intended to shame the wicked (Isa. 3:16-17; 47:1-3).

A Study of 1 Timothy 2:9-10

Paul wrote, **"In like manner, that women adorn themselves in modest apparel, with shamefastness and sobriety; not with braided hair, and gold or pearls or costly raiment; but (which becometh women professing godliness) through good works"** (1 Tim. 2:9-10). The word "modest" comes from *kosmio* which Thayer defines "to put in order, arrange, make ready, well arranged, seemly, modest, and decent." Trench says, "The well-ordering is not of dress and demeanor only, but of the inner life, uttering in deed and expressing itself in the outward conversation." Arndt and Gingrich define the word "make beautiful or attractive spiritually, religiously, morally . . . adorn, do credit to." Paul's statement proves there was modest apparel in that day, which God commanded, and there has been such needed in every age since then. Modest apparel is not determined by specific inches of a hemline, but by common sense and an internal disposition of modesty. Paul also says that women are to adorn themselves "with shamefastness." The Greek word is *aidous*. Thayer defines it: "a sense of shame . . . reverence." He also says it means to dress in such a way that would "always restrain a good man from an unworthy act." It is important to point out that a godly attitude precedes and prevents a shameful act. Can it be said that those who display their bodies so as to excite lust in others have the quality of "shamefastness"? Paul also says a woman is to dress with "sobriety." Arndt and Gingrich says the Greek word *sophrosunes* means "reasonableness, rationality, mental soundness, good judgment, moderation, self-control . . . especially as a feminine virtue, decency, chastity." Trench says the word means ". . . that habitual inner self-government, with its constant rein on all the passions and desires, which would hinder the temptation to these from arising." Notice also that Christian women are not to "adorn" themselves "with braided hair, and gold or pearls, or costly raiment." Paul is not teaching it is a sin for a Christian woman to braid her hair or wear gold or pearls or expensive clothes. The point is, don't let that be the way you seek to truly beautify yourself. Seek to beautify yourself through godliness and good works. Seek **"the beauty of holiness"** (1 Chron. 16:29 KJV). It is much more important for a woman to adorn herself with holiness and godliness. A truly godly man will seek such!

A Study of 1 Peter 3:1-6

In these six verses Peter gives instruction to Christian wives. Notice the value of "chaste behavior." It can make one's influence good and positive. Likewise, improper behavior (e.g. immodest apparel) can have an adverse effect. In verses 3-4 Peter reiterates what Paul said. A Christian woman's emphasis should not be one's outward adornment (i.e. arranging the hair, wearing gold, or putting on apparel), rather, it should be beautifying one's inner person. Some preachers have taken this passage and taught that it is a sin for a woman to wear gold jewelry. If that is true, it is also a sin for a woman to put on clothes. That is ridiculous! The adornment that greatly pleases God is **"the incorruptible apparel of a meek and quiet spirit, which is in the sight of God of great price."** Peter says, "For after this manner aforetime the holy women also, who hoped in God, adorned themselves, being in subjection to their own husbands."

In my dating years, I dated several women. One time I called Barbara and asked her out on a date. I figured she would say no, but she said yes. When she said yes, I almost fainted. Barbara was drop-dead gorgeous with a Playboy-type body. No joke. She was one of the most beautiful women I have ever seen. I enjoyed the date, but her spiritual depth was nonexistent. It was evident she did not love the Lord and did not have **"the beauty of holiness."** She was not the type of girl that would help take me to heaven. Proverbs 31:30 states, **"Grace is deceitful, and beauty is vain; But a woman that feareth Jehovah, she shall be praised."** Barbara definitely had grace and tremendous physical beauty, but she did not fear Jehovah. Therefore, she did not deserve praise.

Women Need To Realize the Power of Their Dress

Women need to be taught that men in general are stimulated by sight. When a woman dresses immodestly, she is setting out temptation to men. Jesus warned, **"But I say unto you, that every one that looketh on a woman to lust after her hath committed adultery in his heart"** (Matt. 5:28). A man sins when he lusts (i.e. has evil desire) on a woman. But, when a woman dresses provocatively and causes a man to lust on her, she is guilty of sin and has also contributed to his sin. Paul said, "Neither be partaker of other men's sins" (1 Tim. 5:22). Though lust is inexcusable on the man's part, if the woman by her apparel or conduct has encouraged it, she shares the guilt. There is definitely a twofold responsibility here! In 2 Samuel 11:2 David was walking on his own roof "and from the roof he saw a woman bathing: and the woman was very beautiful to look upon." David had the right to walk on his own roof. This may be teaching that Bathsheba was in the wrong place. You can be in the right place and be tempted to do the wrong thing.   Notice the text says David "saw." There is tremendous power in seeing and looking. In Proverbs 7:10 we discover **"a woman with the attire of a harlot"** was able to seduce a young man into sexual sin. The way a woman dresses is powerful! Mary Quant was the designer of the mini-skirt. When she was asked why she designed the mini-skirt, here is exactly what she said: "I did it in order to seduce a man to bed." It is no wonder the morals of America are in trouble.

Christians Must Be Transformed Not Conformed to the World

Paul wrote, **"And be not fashioned according to this world: but be ye transformed by the renewing of your mind, that ye may prove what is the good and acceptable and perfect will of God"** (Rom. 12:2). Notice it is through our minds first that we decide to be transformed. Jesus warned us that if we cause a weaker brother to stumble, it will be "woe" unto us (Matt. 18:6-7). The word "woe" means "great sorrow, grief, and misery are coming upon you." Paul said, **"That no man put a stumbling block in his brother's way, or an occasion of falling"** (Rom. 14:13). In Romans 13:13 Paul wrote, "Let us walk becomingly, as in the day; not in reveling and drunkenness, not in chambering and wantonness, not in strife and jealousy." The word "wantonness" is from the Greek *aselgeia* which is defined by Arndt and Gingrich: "follow the inclination to sensuality especially of sexual excess, indecent conduct . . . licentious desires." Here again self-control is called for to avoid a stimulation toward sexual excess by practicing modest concealment. If one's inner disposition honors these God-given directives, there will be no external display to invite sexual excess. In Galatians 5:19-21 Paul gives a list of sins which will keep people out of heaven. One of those sins listed is "lasciviousness." It is the same Greek word *aselgeia* which is found in Romans 13:13. It is interesting that Webster defines the word "tending to excite lustful desires." Whatever tends to produce evil thoughts or excite lustful desires is "lasciviousness" and is condemned as a work of the flesh in Galatians 5.

The Fruit of Immodest Dress

Jesus said, **"Therefore, by their fruits ye shall know them"** (Matt. 7:20). What is the fruit of immodest dress? The fruit is lust, fornications, adultery, rape, lowering the morals of our nation, babies born to unwed mothers, etc. Immodest apparel is wrong because of the fruit it produces.

A good honest test of God's principles was supplied by Paul K. Williams, who wrote of the behavior of some women on board the Santa Maria when Portugese rebels took over the ship. Immediately upon the ship being boarded by the swarthy rebels, these ladies of the world stopped wearing any shorts or halters or going to the swimming pool. The rebels aboard that ship gave them an instant insight as to what constitutes modest apparel! These women did not need a course in training from a Christian university nor a session with mature elders in His kingdom to determine what modest apparel is. Those circumstances quickly resulted in a personal application of what these women of the world already knew! Hence, just be honest with yourself. Then a personal application of 1 Thessalonians 5:21-22 would be appropriate: **"Prove all things; hold fast that which is good: abstain from every form of evil."**

The Sin of Pornography

Former U. S. Surgeon General, Dr. C. Everett Koop, declared pornography a "crushing public health problem . . . a clear and present danger . . . blatantly anti-human . . . We must oppose it as we oppose all violence and prejudice." J. Edgar Hoover, ex-head of the FBI, said, "It is impossible to determine the amount of harm to impressionable teenagers and to assess the volume of sex crimes attributable to pornography." Ted Bundy maintained that "drug store soft-core pornography" helped change him into a brutal mass murderer of over thirty women and girls. Dr. Judith Reisman states, "Pornography bears an enormous responsibility for the spiraling rate of divorce, venereal disease, abortion, as well as new and deadly forms of sex crimes against women and children." Pornography promotes lust. Peter said, **"Beloved, I beseech you as sojourners and pilgrims, to abstain from fleshly lusts, which war against the soul"** (1 Pet. 2:11). Magazines like Playboy degrade women into mere sex objects. It also degrades the act of sex. That which God said is pure, holy, honorable, and undefiled in marriage (Heb. 13:4) is degraded to the level of animal actions. The main function of pornography is to promote the sexual arousal in its viewers. To arouse desires that can only be rightly fulfilled in marriage must be taken by Christians to be wrong and sinful.

Pornography makes a cultural statement. Behind the pictures there has always stood a philosophy. What is being sold is not only nude pictures but a hedonistic lifestyle. Immediate self-gratification takes precedence over the common good; personal pleasure comes before the will of God (Eccl. 12:13-14; 1 Pet. 4:2). A few years ago the promoters of pornography prophesied that if we would get rid of our inhibitions and sexual hang-ups that human relationships would improve. They said there would be more love and less violence among us. Well, the evidence is now in! The sexual revolution has done just the opposite of what its advocates claimed. In 1996 the Attorney General's Report said pornography leads to violent crime. In a study performed by the Michigan State Police, researchers reported that in fully two-thirds of all sex-related crimes, the perpetrator either had just read pornography or had pornographic materials in his possession. In another study conducted among convicted rapists in Southern California, a medical researcher reported that 57 percent of the study's control group admitted that sex crimes were premeditated to act out behavior in pornography that they had read or viewed. Gary Bishop, a convicted killer, said, "Pornography was a determining factor in my downfall." FBI researchers did a profile of a rapist. They said, "The rapist collected Playboy, then Penthouse magazines . . . and dreamed of rape. Then he slipped over the threshold of fantasy into the reality of sexual assault." Roger Miller, a police officer, said whenever he went into the home of a sex-crime suspect, he almost always found pornography. Joe Smith, a detective, said, "Every time we search the home of a sex crime suspect, the house is filled with this stuff." In 1988, Gregory Goben, a married minster with two sons, was convicted of five rapes. He said his actions were the result of viewing pornographic material. We are not what we think we are, rather we are what we think (Prov. 23:7). If we think about evil, we will become evil! If we think about good, we will become good! It is just that simple. Edward Gibbon wrote *The Decline and Fall of the Roman Empire.* In his book he gives five main reasons why Rome was destroyed. One was an obsession with sex and sensuality. Pornography promotes sex and sensuality in a bad way. Christians need to stay away from this terrible sin.

The Sin of Inhibition Within Marriage

There are some things that are right at certain times and wrong at other times. For example, taking drugs can be right when trying to lessen the pain of surgery. Taking drugs without a prescription or abusing prescription drugs is wrong. That is a form of drunkenness which is sin (Gal. 5:19-21). Speeding is wrong the majority of the time. But, if your wife is having a baby, and you need to get her to the hospital as soon as possible, you might need to speed. Sometimes police officers will give you a careful police escort. Nudity is basically wrong. But, nudity has a place, and that place is within marriage. Titus 2:4 says that the older women are to **"train the younger women to love their husbands."** The word "love" is from *phileo* which means in context "to show physical signs of affection." Proverbs 5:19 says, **"Let her breasts satisfy thee at all times."** In 1 Cor. 7:4 Paul said, **"The wife hath not power over her own body but the husband."** The Song of Solomon discusses the intimate physical love-making between husband and wife. It is quite graphic. Read it! Hebrews 13:4 states, **"Let marriage be had in honor among all, and let the bed be undefiled: for fornicators and adulterers God will judge."**

Joseph and Lois Bird wrote, "Nudity between husband and wife has nothing, repeat, nothing to do with the virtue of modesty. In the intimacy of marriage, undressing for each other should be as natural and unselfconscious as a shared laugh or a mutual prayer" (*The Freedom of Sexual Love*, p.104).

Joseph Dillow said, "Because the world tends to flaunt the body and sex, it is natural for Christians to associate inhibition with Christian modesty and the 'sacredness' of sex. Actually, based on the Song of Solomon and the rest of the Bible, inhibition outside marriage reflects Christian modesty but within marriage reflects the pattern of this world. The world system cheapens and degrades sex, but paradoxically, within marriage many women are still inhibited. Because the world exploits the female body to the ultimate, some Christian women desire to be the opposite of the world. The world exposes the body, so they conceal it. They are not going to be like the nasty women in the Playboy centerfold and reveal their bodies to their husbands or do the things 'those girls' do." Dillow says inhibitions "are frequently the cause of much tension and resentment on the part of the husband." Again he says, "Inhibition is insisting on an authority that you no longer have and thus is sin."

Conclusion

God is concerned with what we wear. To say "It's nobody's business what I put on my body" is pure folly! The Christian ethic is to dress modestly and to please God (1 Cor. 10:31). When faced with the problem of what to wear, may I suggest (1) Prayerfully and honestly consider whether your adornment reflects godliness and "the beauty of holiness" and (2) Seek counsel from those who are mature in the faith. Moses wrote, **"Remember the days of old, consider the years of many generations: Ask thy father, and he will show thee; Thine elders, and they will tell thee"** (Deut. 32:7).

Several ladies gave me this four question checklist in determining what to wear. (1) Would God approve of this outfit? (2) Would this portray me as a godly woman? (3) Would this look immodest on my mother? (4) Would the preacher approve?

For Thought or Discussion

1 When it comes to attire, what attitude should Christians have?
2 What does 1 Corinthians 10:31 teach?
3 What did God do about the clothing of Adam and Eve? Why?
4 How did the Old Testament priests dress?
5 How are Christian women to dress? (1 Timothy 2:9-10).
6 What type of beauty should we all seek? (1 Chron. 16:29)
7 How is a Christian woman not to adorn herself?
8 How is a Christian woman to adorn herself?
9 What does Proverbs 31:30 teach?
10 (T or F) A woman can contribute to the sin of a man lusting on her.
11 (T or F) One can be in the right place and be tempted to sin.
12 What did Mary Quant say about the miniskirt?
13 Define the word "woe."
14 Define the Greek word *aselgeia*.
15 What is the fruit of immodest dress?
16 What lifestyle does Playboy magazine portray?
17 What does pornography promote and degrade?
18 What did Edward Gibbon do? Significance?
19 (T or F) Nudity is always wrong and sinful.
20 What does the Song of Solomon teach

emphatically?

21 (T or F) Nudity in marriage has nothing to do with the virtue of modesty.

22 (T or F) Inhibitions inside marriage reflect Christian modesty.

23 (T or F) Inhibition inside marriage is insisting on authority one does not have.

24 (T or F) It is wise to ask older Christians for help in what to wear.

25 What are four good questions to ask when deciding what to wear?

26 What did Peter say that Christians are to abstain from? (1 Pet. 2:11) Why?

Chapter 12-Self-Discipline

When I was an eight-year-old boy, I did not like to take a bath. That is probably typical of young boys. One time my father told me to go take a bath. I did not want to do it, but I knew I had to do what my father told me. I went into the bathroom, locked the door, and filled up the tub with water , then swished my hand in the water, and read a comic book. After a few minutes, I drained the tub and came out and headed toward my room. My father noticed that I did not use a wash rag, so he asked me, "John, did you take a bath?" I did not lie to him. I said, "No." He replied, "Get in there and take a bath." Admittedly, I was a young boy. Today, I gladly take a shower, sometimes two a day. But, many times as a youngster, we think and feel and act like a child. We do childish things. As we grow into adulthood, we learn that we must do what is needed done whether we want to or not! This is what Christian Ethics is all about (1 Cor. 13:11). It is learning to live as the Lord would have us live. It is practicing self-discipline and self-denial and living "unto Him" (2 Cor. 5:15).

Elihu said, "He (i.e. God) openeth also their ear to instruction" (Job 36:10). The word "instruction" in Hebrew is *musar* which refers to "moral discipline, the strenuous cultivation of the righteous life." Webster defines "self-discipline" as "orderly conduct resulting from self-control." A practical definition of self-discipline is "making yourself do what is right; doing what needs to be done without having to be told."

Life on This Earth Is Short

Job said, "My days are swifter than a weaver's shuttle" (Job 7:6) and "My days are swifter than a post (i.e. runner): they flee away" (Job 9:25) and **"Man that is born of woman, Is of few days and full of trouble"** (Job 14:1). Moses wrote, **"The days of our years are threescore and ten, or even by reason of strength fourscore years; Yet is their pride but labor and sorrow; For it is soon gone and we fly away"** (Psa. 90:10). The apostle Paul taught we are only on this earth "for the moment" (2 Cor. 4:17). Twice Peter said we are only here on this earth for "a little while" (1 Peter 1:6; 5:10). My grandmother said, "You turn around and you've had a life." How true!

What Can We Learn from These Scriptures?

Since we are not on this earth for very long, Moses wrote, **"So teach us to number our days, that we may get us a heart of wisdom"** (Psa. 90:12). Moses also wrote, **"Oh that they were wise, that they understood this, that they would consider their latter end!"** (Deut. 32:29). David said, **"Jehovah, make me to know mine end, and the measure of my days, what it is; let me know how frail I am"** (Psa. 39:4). We can be wise if we realize we are not on this earth for very long and live for the Lord! Wisdom will look at the "latter end" (i.e. where we will spend eternity) and therefore, we will live accordingly. Solomon said, **"Rejoice, O young man, in thy youth, and let thy heart cheer thee in the days of thy youth, and walk in the ways of thy heart, and in** the sight of thine eyes; but know thou, that for all these things God will bring thee into judgment" (Eccl. 11:9). Solomon also said, "And the dust returneth to the earth as it was, and the spirit returneth unto God who gave it" (Eccl. 12:7). Again he wrote, "For God will bring every work into judgment, with every hidden thing, whether it be good or whether it be evil" (Eccl. 12:14). Paul wrote, "For we must all be made manifest before the judgment-seat of Christ; that each one may receive the things done in the body, according to what he hath done, whether it be good or bad" (2 Cor. 5:10). Where we spend eternity depends upon what we have done "in the body." Hebrews 9:27 clearly teaches we will not get a second chance.

Self-Denial

One scholar pointed out that as far as recorded Scripture is concerned, Jesus taught more about self-denial than He did anything else. He gave many parables on the kingdom, but they dealt with different aspects of the kingdom. The seven recorded texts that deal with self-denial are: Matthew 10:34-39; Matthew 16:24-25; Mark 8:34-35; Luke 9:23-25; Luke 14:26-27; Luke 17:33; and John 12:25. I will only quote one of these texts. Matthew 16:24-25 states, **"Then said Jesus unto his disciples, If any man would come after me, let him deny himself, and take up his cross, and follow me. For whosoever would save his life shall lose it: and whosoever shall lose his life for my sake shall find it."** The verb "deny" in Matthew 16:24 comes from the Greek word *aparneomai* which means "to deny utterly." This verb is used to convey the most conclusive denial. This means that one must live his life without a single thread of self-centered thought. One must live a life devoted exclusively to Jesus and His work. Our will, our wants, and our desires must become subservient to the Lord's will. We must be willing to give up anything or anyone for the sake of Jesus. To deny oneself is to renounce the self as the dominant element in life. It is to place God's will before one's own self-will. God's will must be first in our lives. Cranfield said, "To deny oneself is to disown, not just one's sins, but one's self, to turn away from the idolatry of self-centeredness."

Jesus said we are to pray, **"Thy will be done"** (Matt. 6:10). Peter said we are to live "to the will of God" (1 Pet. 4:2). Paul said, **"And he died for all, that they that live should no longer live unto themselves, but unto him who for their sakes died and rose again"** (2 Cor. 5:15). Paul also said, **"Denying ungodliness and worldly lusts, we should live soberly and righteously and godly in this present world"** (Titus 2:12). In the Book of Revelation those who overcame Satan did so because "they loved not their life even unto death" (Rev. 12:11). Ecclesiastes 12:13 states, **"This is the end of the matter; all hath been heard: Fear God, and keep his commandments; for this is the whole duty of man."** It is not our wills and our desires that are important. We must give up what we want for what the Lord wants!

Jesus said we are to take up our "cross" and follow Him. The word "cross" refers to whatever burdens one might have to bear and endure in this life for the cause of Jesus. The cross of Jesus meant extreme pain, suffering, and agony. He offered up to the Father **"strong crying and tears"** (Heb. 5:7-8) three times asking for its removal. But, the attitude of Jesus was: **"Nevertheless**

not my will, but thine, be done" (Luke 22:42). We must have this same mind-set! We must endure any pain, any hardship, any suffering for the Lord's sake. It will not be easy. It was not easy for Jesus (Heb. 12:1-3). We are told to follow in His steps (1 Pet. 2:21) and to walk even as He walked (1 John 2:6). **If the life of Jesus is not our pattern, the death of Jesus will not be our pardon!** But, we must always remember that we have the promise of God: He will reward us! Romans 8:18 states, "For I reckon that the sufferings of this present time are not worthy to be compared with the glory which shall be revealed to us-ward." Hebrews 11:6 states, "And without faith it is impossible to be well-pleasing unto him; for he that cometh to God must believe that he is, and that he is a rewarder of them that diligently seek after him." God demands that we believe one day He will reward us! If we don't believe that, the verse says we do not have faith and cannot be well-pleasing to Him. The Christian ethic is that we must deny ourselves now for a short time, so we can reap Heaven for all eternity. As the great song writer Oliver Cooper wrote, "Heaven will surely be worth it all!" Amen!

Biblical Examples of Self-Discipline

Joseph was tempted to commit adultery with Potiphar's wife. He could have reasoned that he was far away from his family, his brothers had mistreated him, and that he was entitled to have some pleasure. But, he was true to God. He practiced self-denial and said no to the pleasures of sin. He told Potiphar's wife, **"How then can I do this great wickedness, and sin against God?"** (Gen. 39:9).

Moses practiced self-denial. He **"refused to be called the son of Pharaoh's daughter; choosing rather to share ill treatment with the people of God, than to enjoy the pleasures of sin for a season; accounting the reproach of Christ greater riches than the treasures of Egypt"** (Heb. 11:24-26).

Daniel practiced self-denial. Daniel 1:8 states, "But Daniel purposed in his heart that he would not defile himself with the king's dainties, nor with the wine which he drank." Even though he was tempted, Daniel had a mind-set to obey God.

Shadrach, Meshach, and Abednego were willing to be thrown into the fiery furnace and die before they would worship the golden image Nebuchadnezzar had set up (Dan. 3:13-18). They chose death over turning their backs to the Lord.

The apostle Paul practiced self-denial. He said, **"But I buffet my body, and bring it into bondage: lest by any means, after that I have preached to others, I myself should be rejected (i.e. be a reprobate)"** (1 Cor. 9:27).

Biblical Examples of Non Self-Discipline

Judges 16:1 states, **"And Samson went to Gaza, and saw there a harlot, and went in unto her."** He did not deny himself "the pleasures of sin." Proverbs 5-7 teaches emphatically the sin of having sex with a prostitute or the "strange woman." The word "strange" means "unlawful." In the text it is any woman you do not have any business being with! In Judges 16:4 we read, **"He loved a woman in the valley of Sorek, whose**

name was Delilah." Samson may have been a physical giant, but he did not have the moral strength to resist the influence of the Philistine idolater Delilah. He failed to follow the instruction of Proverbs 31:30. He should have sought a godly woman, but he went after the ungodly Delilah. He was selfish and self-centered and failed to practice self-denial. Again Paul said, **"Denying ungodliness and worldly lusts, we should live soberly and righteously and godly in this present world"** (Titus 2:12).

Saul was not a priest. Only priests were to offer sacrifices. In 1 Samuel 13 the Israelite army was camped at Gilgal preparing for a battle against the Philistines. Saul waited seven days for Samuel to show up to offer the sacrifice before the battle. On the seventh day, Saul thought he could wait no longer so he offered the sacrifice himself. "As soon as he had made an end of offering the burnt offering, behold Samuel came" (1 Sam. 13:10). Samuel said, "What hast thou done?" (1 Sam. 13:11). 1 Samuel 13:13 states, "And Samuel said to Saul, Thou hast done foolishly; thou hast not kept the commandment of Jehovah thy God, which he commanded thee." Sadly, Saul did not practice self-discipline. He should have made himself wait. He knew he was not allowed to offer the sacrifice. He acted "foolishly" and lost his kingdom. Had he waited, Samuel would have arrived "according to the set time that Samuel had appointed" (1 Sam. 13:8).

When David died, God told Solomon, "Ask what I shall give thee" (1 Kings 3:5). Solomon asked for wisdom. God told Solomon because he did not ask for long life, riches, or the life of his enemies, He would give him not only wisdom but also riches and honor (1 Kings 3:13). Solomon was blessed by God. God told him, "There hath been none like thee before thee, neither after thee shall any arise like unto thee" (1 King 3:12). One of the saddest verses in the Bible is 1 Kings 11:4. It states, **"For it came to pass, when Solomon was old, that his wives turned away his heart after other gods; and his heart was not perfect with Jehovah his God, as was the heart of David his father."** How could Solomon with all that wisdom turn his heart away from God? Yes, he allowed his wives to turn his heart away. But, there is a much more fundamental reason. It is one thing to know what is right—it is another thing to do that which is right! Solomon knew what was right. He just failed to do that which was right. Solomon did not practice self-discipline. Self-discipline is when you make yourself do that which is right!

One of the shortest verses in the Bible carries a powerful message. Jesus said, **"Remember Lot's wife"** (Luke 17:32). There is a great lesson we can learn from this story! Lot and his family were told, "Look not behind thee . . . lest thou be consumed" (Gen. 19:17). However, Lot's wife "looked back from behind him, and she became a pillar of salt" (Gen. 19:26). She did not practice self-discipline. She had a simple command "look not behind thee" and she was disobedient. She should have made herself do what she was told to do. The main lesson we must learn from this account is that sin always brings punishment; disobedience always brings God's chastisement (Heb. 2:2-3). Lot's wife had a choice-either to obey or disobey. Sadly, she did not have the self-discipline and wisdom to obey. She was also told she would be "consumed" if she disobeyed. Righteousness and self-discipline is a choice. John wrote, **"He that doeth righteousness is righteous"** (1 John 3;7). Jesus said, **"Why call ye me, Lord, Lord, and do not the things which I say?"** (Luke 6:46).

Conclusion

Self-discipline is up to us! Joshua said many years ago, **"Choose you this day whom ye will serve"** (Joshua 24:15). Right action is a choice. God will not force us to make the right choice. He leaves that up to us. If we are wise, we will use self-discipline to make the right choice. Moses said, **"See I have set before thee this day life and good, and death and evil . . . therefore choose life, that thou mayest live"** (Deut. 30:15, 19). God wants us to make the right choice but He leaves that to us. Peter told the Jews on the Day of Pentecost, "Save yourselves from this crooked generation" (Acts 2:40). The person who goes to heaven will be the one who practiced self-discipline and did what God told him to do! We are not saying we can earn our way into heaven. That is impossible. But, we can and must be faithful! Wise people hear and obey (Matt. 7:24-27). John said, **"He that doeth righteousness is righteous"** (1 John 3:7). Hebrews 3:14 states, "For we are become partakers of Christ, if we hold fast the beginning of our confidence firm unto the end."

For Thought or Discussion

1 (T or F) The Christian ethic is to mature spiritually and put away childish things.
2 Define "self-discipline."

3 How long did Moses say our lifetime is on this earth?

4 From Psalms 90:12 how do we get wisdom?

5 From Deut. 32:29 how do we get wisdom?

6 What is the promise of Ecclesiastes 12:14?

7 What is the importance of the phrase "in the body" in 2 Cor. 5:10?

8 How many recorded texts deal with self-denial in the New Testament?

9 What does it mean to deny self?

10 What did Peter say we are to live to? Scripture?

11 What is a Christian no longer to live unto? Scripture?

12 What did Paul say we are to deny? (Titus 2:12)

13 What is the whole duty of man? Scripture?

14 Describe the cross of Jesus.

15 (T or F) It was easy for Jesus to obey His Father.

16 (T or F) It will be easy for us to obey God.

17 What is the promise of Hebrews 11:6 to help us in tough times?

18 What are some biblical examples of self-discipline?

19 How did Samson not show self-discipline?

20 Describe Solomon's fundamental problem as it relates to self-discipline.

21 What lesson can we learn from Lot's wife?

22 (T or F) Righteousness is a choice.

23 Who is righteous? Scripture?

24 What was the sermon Moses preached in Deuteronomy 30:15, 19?

25 How can we become partakers of Christ? Scripture?

Chapter 13- Discipleship

If we choose to follow in the steps of Jesus (1 Pet. 2:21) and walk even as He walked (1 John 2:6), then we can be truly a disciple of Jesus. The word "disciple" is from *mathetes* which means "one who follows one's teaching; one who imitates their teacher." Some qualities that should characterize the disciples of Jesus will be presented in this chapter. These qualities are for all disciples and not just for an elite few.

The Way of Suffering

In the Gospel of Mark there are three texts that deal with the suffering of Jesus (Mark 8:31-33; 9:30-32; 10:32-34). Immediately after each text, Jesus talks about the cost of discipleship (Mark 8:34-9:1; 9:33-37; 10:35-45). Jesus is teaching that discipleship involves suffering for the Lord. The twelve disciples were having great difficulty in accepting the idea that God's Messiah should be humiliated by His enemies and have to suffer death on the cross. Jesus told them, **"If they persecuted me, they will also persecute you"** (John 15:20). In Matthew 10:17 Jesus warned them saying, "But beware of men: for they will deliver you up to councils, and in their synagogues **they will scourge you**." Again in Matthew 24:9 Jesus also warned them saying, "Then shall they deliver you up unto tribulation, **and shall kill you**: and ye shall be hated of all nations for my name's sake." It has been said, "To be forewarned is to be forearmed." Jesus wanted His disciples to know ahead of time they were going to suffer and expect it so when it came, the suffering would not catch them off-guard and unprepared. This hard and tough principle of suffering set forth in the example and teaching of Jesus is a necessary step in the victorious life for all His disciples in every age. Peter wrote, **"Beloved, think it not strange concerning the fiery trial among you, which cometh upon you to prove you, as though a strange thing happened unto you"** (1 Pet. 4:12). Paul said, **"Yea, and all that would live godly in Christ Jesus shall suffer persecution"** (2 Tim. 3:12). Paul also said, "That through many tribulations we must enter into the kingdom of God" (Acts 14:22).

The Way of Faithfulness

Jesus said, **"If ye abide in my word, then are ye truly my disciples"** (John 8:31). He also said, "Why call ye me Lord, Lord, and do not the things which I say?" (Luke 6:46). Again He said, "Not everyone that saith unto me, Lord, Lord, shall enter into the kingdom of heaven; but he that doeth the will of my Father who is in heaven" (Matt. 7:21). True discipleship involves faithfulness characterized by obedience. Jesus said, "Be thou faithful unto death, and I will give thee the crown of life" (Rev. 2:10). The way of faithfulness is not always easy, but it can and must be done! To abide in His word, we must be obedient to His commandments. Jesus said, **"If ye love me, ye will keep my commandments"** (John 14:15). He also said, **"Ye are my friends, if ye do the things which I command you"** (John 15:14). The apostle John wrote, "He that saith, I know him, and keepeth not his commandments is a liar, and the truth is not in him" (1 John 2:4).

The Way of Love

Jesus said, **"By this shall all men know that ye are my disciples, if ye have love one to another"** (John 13:35). True discipleship is proven by the way we love one another. The word "love" is from *agape* which means "active unconditional good-will; seeking another's best interests; genuine care and concern." John said, **"If a man say, I love God, and hateth his brother, he is a liar: for he that loveth not his brother whom he hath seen, cannot love God whom he hath not seen"** (1 John 4:20). Paul said, "Let all that ye do be done in love" (1 Cor. 16:14). Again he said, "And above all these things put on love, which is the bond of perfectness" (Col. 3:14). Peter said, "Above all things being fervent in your love among yourselves" (1 Pet. 4:8). The way of love is sharing. It is helping those in need. John wrote, **"But whoso hath the world's goods, and beholdeth his brother in need, and shutteth up his compassion from him, how doth the love of God abide in him?"** (1 John 4:17). One writer correctly observed that love and self-denial are the two great characteristics of the Christian life as taught by Jesus.

The Way of Bearing Fruit

Jesus said, **"Herein is my Father glorified, that ye bear much fruit; and so shall ye be my disciples"** (John 15:8). The disciples of Christ are commanded to "bear much fruit." Notice not just "fruit" but "much fruit." This means that we must take our work for the

Lord very seriously! Jesus also said, **"Even so let your light shine before men; that they may see your good works, and glorify your Father who is in heaven"** (Matt. 5:16). We have been "created in Christ Jesus for good works" (Eph. 2:10). We are told to be "rich in good works" (1 Tim. 6:18), "zealous of good works" (Titus 2:14), and "maintain good works" (Titus 3:8). We are to "consider one another to provoke unto love and good works" (Heb. 10:24). Bearing fruit is any good work performed for the Lord. Every prayer we offer, every tract and book we give away, every meal we give to the needy, and every dollar we give to the Lord is bearing fruit.

The Way of Humility

"Humility" is "the absence of pride or self-assertion." On at least three distinct occasions Jesus enunciated the paradoxical principle that **"whoever exalts himself will be humbled, and whoever humbles himself will be exalted"** (Matt. 23:12; Luke 14:11; 18:14). The Pharisees did their deeds "before men, to be seen of them" and "that they might have glory of men" (Matt. 6:1-2). They have received their reward. We are to seek our reward from our Father without fanfare! The scribes loved "to have salutations in the marketplaces, and chief seats in the synagogues, and chief places at feasts" (Mark 12:38-39). The source of true humility is a consciousness of the presence and majesty of God. Such a consciousness will cause one, like the tax-collector, to "beat his breast" and say, "God, be merciful to me a sinner!" It will also inspire one to give himself in unselfish devotion to the needs of his fellowman. Proverbs 15:33 states, **"Before honor goeth humility."**

Proverbs 22:4 says, **"The reward of humility and the fear of Jehovah are riches, and honor, and life."**

The Way of Forgiveness

As Jesus was dying on the cross He prayed, **"Father, forgive them; for they know not what they do"** (Luke 23:34). Jesus set the example that we are to follow (1 Pet. 2:21; 1 John 2:6). In the Model Prayer we read, **"For if ye forgive men their trespasses, your heavenly Father will also forgive you. But if ye forgive not men their trespasses, neither will your Father forgive your trespasses"** (Matt. 6:14-15). One preacher said, "God forgives only the forgiving." It is sometimes argued that one cannot forgive unless the offender repents. It is true that Jesus said, "If thy brother sin, rebuke him; and if he repent, forgive him" (Luke 17:3). What if the offender does not repent? Answer: he cannot be forgiven. Yes, the act of forgiveness is incomplete without repentance followed by forgiveness and restoration. But, like Jesus we can and we must have the willingness to forgive and the spirit of forgiveness in our hearts regardless of what the offender does or does not do. Forgiveness is more an attitude than an act; at least the attitude precedes the act.

The Way of Service

Jesus said, **"Even as the Son of man came not to be ministered unto, but to minister, and to give his life as a ransom for many"** (Matt. 20:28). Jesus took upon Himself "the form of a servant" (Phil. 2:7). Washing feet in the first century was a dirty job. It was usually performed by the lowest servant. After He washed the disciples' feet, He said, **"Know ye what I have done to you? Ye call me, Teacher, and, Lord: and ye say well; for so I am. If I then, the Lord and the Teacher, have washed your feet, ye also ought to wash one another's feet. For I have given you an example, that ye also should do as I have done to you"** (John 13:12-15). Christians should be willing to perform the job that no one else wants to do. One time a husband said, "When we have a baby, I am never going to change a diaper." Is that following the example of Jesus? One time a husband said, "I am never going to wash a dish." Again, is that being a disciple of Jesus? Jesus said, **"He that is greatest among you shall be your servant"** (Matt. 23:11). Greatness in the Kingdom is not determined by barking orders and issuing commands. Greatness is demonstrated by being a servant. Discipleship is the way of service to others. Jesus sets forth the place of service most pointedly in the parable of the last judgment (Matt. 25:31-46). The blessing or curse was dependent upon their service to their fellow man. The service rendered was in the area of everyday needs of the common people: feeding the hungry, taking in the stranger, clothing the naked, and visiting those in prison. It was not spectacular service. Just giving someone a drink of cold water was true discipleship (Matt. 10:42). Jesus said that taking care of those in need was taking of Him.

The Way of the Cross

Jesus said, **"Greater love hath no man than this, that a man lay down his life for his friends"** (John 15:13). Paul said that Jesus "existing in the form of God, counted not the being on an equality with God a thing to be grasped, but emptied himself, taking the form of a servant, being made in the likeness of men: and being found in fashion as a man, he humbled himself, becoming obedient even unto death, yea, the death of the cross" (Phil. 2:6-8). Jesus asked three times for the cross to be removed from Him (Matt. 26: 39-44). God the Father said no every time. The Hebrew writer recorded that Jesus **"offered up prayers and supplications with strong crying and tears unto him that was able to save him from death"** (Heb. 5:7). It definitely was not easy for Jesus to suffer and die on the cross! It was extremely hard! It was excruciating pain! But, Jesus yielded His will to the Father's will and said three times, "Nevertheless not my will, but thine, be done" (Luke 22:42). What does it mean to take up our cross and follow Jesus? It means the self, with selfish motives, will no longer be the center around which one builds his life. The will and purposes of God must become dominant in his life. This will mean a radical reorientation of life. Love will be directed toward God and neighbor rather than to one's self. Paul said, **"I have been crucified with Christ; it is no longer I who live, but Christ who lives in me"** (Gal. 2:20). Six times Jesus said, "For whosoever would save his life shall lose it; and whosoever shall lose his life for my sake and the gospel's shall save it" (Mark 8:35; cf. Matt. 10:39; 16:25; Luke 9:24; 17:33; John 12:25). Our desires, our wants, and our wills must be subservient to what the Lord would have us to do! We are going to follow the example of Christ. Paul said, "For Christ also pleased not himself" (Rom. 15:3). Jesus said, "For I do always the things that are pleasing to him" (John 8:29).

The Way of the Lord

The disciple of Jesus should walk in the way of the Lord. Jesus said, **"Ye therefore shall be perfect, as your heavenly Father is perfect"** (Matt. 5:48). Paul said, "Be ye therefore imitators of God" (Eph. 5:1). Peter said, "But like as he who called you is holy, be ye yourselves also holy in all manner of living; because it is written, Ye shall be holy; for I am holy" (1 Peter 1:15-16). Just as Jesus came into the world to reveal the Father (Matt. 11:27; Luke 10:22; John 1:18; 12:45; 14:9; 17:6), His disciples are sent into the world to reveal Jesus (Matt. 28:18-20; Mark 16:15-16; Acts 1:8; John 15:27; 2 Tim. 2:2). Paul said, "Be ye imitators of me, even as I also am of Christ" (1 Cor. 11:1).

The initial invitation by Jesus to Peter and Andrew and Matthew was, "Follow me" (Matt 4:19; 9:9). To the rich young ruler He said, "Sell what you have, and give to the poor . . . and come, follow me" (Matt. 19:21). This was and is His continuing invitation. Peter, on one occasion, said to Jesus: "Lo, we have left all, and have followed thee" (Matt. 19:27). That may not be literally true, but they had left their businesses and, evidently for most of the time, their families. A disciple must be willing to give up anything that might interfere with his following Jesus. This includes not only what he has (Luke 14:33), but also his loved ones and even his own life (Luke 14:26). One pointed question is: Would any merely human teacher venture to make such claims? These claims of Jesus point to His deity! As we seek to follow Jesus, His life and teachings give us the sense of direction we need. He not only provides a pattern of life for us to follow, He gives us the desire and strength to walk in that way, although our walk is admittedly imperfect. Paul wrote, **"For the love of Christ constraineth us; because we thus judge, that one died for all, therefore all died; and he died for all, that they live should no longer live unto themselves, but unto him who for their sakes died and rose again"** (2 Cor. 5:14-15).

The Way of Bible Knowledge

When Jesus was twelve years old, He was in the temple discussing Scripture with the learned teachers (i.e. "doctors" KJV—Luke 2:46). When He was tempted by the Devil three times, He said, "It is written" (Matt. 4:4, 6, 10). Jesus believed in the inspiration of Scripture. In Matthew 5:18, He believed in the inspiration of the individual letters of the Old Testament to the smallest detail. When the Pharisees wanted an answer to the current marriage and divorce controversy, Jesus appealed to the written word of God by saying, "Have ye not read?" (Matt. 19:4). When the Sadducees asked him about the resurrection, **"Jesus answered and said unto them, Ye do err, not knowing the scriptures, nor the power of God"** (Matt. 22:29). Jesus went every week to study the Scriptures "as his custom was" (Luke 4:16). Jesus said the word of God was "truth" (John 17:17) which could set men free (John 8:32).

If we are going to be a true disciple of Jesus, we are going to diligently study the Bible. There is absolutely no substitute for Bible study! Paul said we are **"not to go beyond the things which are written"** (1 Cor. 4:6). The things that Paul wrote "are the commandment of the Lord" (1 Cor. 14:37). We are commanded not to be ignorant "but understand what the will of the Lord is" (Eph. 5:17). This is impossible without serious study. In Acts 17:10-11 we learn that the Bereans **"were more noble than those in Thessalonica, in that they received the word with all readiness of mind, examining the scriptures daily, whether these things were so."** Paul told Timothy to *spoudazo* the Scriptures (2 Tim. 2:15). This Greek word means "to work hard; give maximum effort; do one's best." Do we work hard and give maximum effort in studying the Bible? The written word of God is our guide book to heaven (Acts 20:32). In Revelation 2-3 we discover seven times that the Holy Spirit leads us through the written word of God. Revelation 20:12 states that on the Day of Judgment **"the dead were judged out of the things which were written in the books (i.e. the books of the Bible), according to their works."** Peter said we are to **"grow in knowledge"** (2 Pet. 3:18).

The Way of Giving

John 3:16 states, **"For God so loved the world that he gave."** True love gives! Giving is a very important aspect of love! If husbands love their wives, they will give (Eph. 5:25). If wives love their husbands, they will give (Titus 2:4). Jesus said, **"Give, and it shall be given unto you"** (Luke 6:38). Proverbs 19:17 states, "He that hath pity upon the poor lendeth unto Jehovah, and his good deed will he pay him again." We will be blessed by God if we give to the poor. Psalms 41:1 says, **"Blessed is he that considereth the poor: Jehovah will deliver him in the day of evil."** The righteous man "hath given to the needy" (Psa. 112:9). Not only should we give to the poor and needy, we must give to the Lord!

Paul said, **"He that soweth sparingly shall reap also sparingly; and he that soweth bountifully shall reap also bountifully"** (2 Cor. 9:6). **"God loveth a cheerful giver"** (2 Cor. 9:7). We prove the sincerity of our love through our giving (2 Cor. 8:8, 24). In 1973, my teenage cousin Mark worked construction for me making about $120 per week. One day the conversation of the work crew dealt with giving to the Lord. Mark said, "Twenty dollars a week isn't much to give to a man who died for you." How true! We cannot buy our way into heaven-- that is impossible. But, we can show the Lord we appreciate Him dying for us through our giving. Jesus taught us to lay up treasures in heaven (Matt. 6:19-21). One way to do this is by giving.

Conclusion

To follow Jesus means we must be a disciple. We must imitate the life of Jesus and follow His teachings. We must **"follow his steps"** (1 Pet. 2:21) and **"walk even as he walked"** (1 John 2:6). Christian ethics is conforming one's life to the standards of conduct as set forth by Jesus. It will not always be easy to obey Jesus, but it can and must be done! One day He will reward us. If we do not believe we will be rewarded, we do not have faith and cannot be well-pleasing to God (Heb. 11:6).

For Thought or Discussion

1 Define disciple.
2 How are suffering and discipleship linked in the Gospel of Mark?
3 What problem did the disciples have in Jesus' suffering and dying?

4   (T or F) The disciples were warned they would be scourged and killed.

5   What did Peter and Paul teach about suffering?

6   What does it mean to abide in the words of Jesus?

7   (T or F) The way of faithful obedience is always easy.

8   What proves discipleship in John 13:35?

9   Define *agape* love.

10 What proves discipleship in John 15:8?

11 Define "bear much fruit."

12 Why did the Pharisees do good deeds?

13 How should Christians seek their reward from God?

14 What should we do if one will not repent?

15 According to Matt 20:28 why did Jesus come?

16 Why did Jesus wash the disciples' feet?

17 How is greatness determined in the kingdom?

18 From Hebrews 5:7 what was the attitude of Jesus as He faced the cross?

19 What does it mean to take up our cross and follow Jesus?

20 What does it mean that to save your life you must lose it?

21 (T or F) Following Jesus may cost us our possessions and life.

22 Why should we no longer live unto ourselves? Scripture?

23 What did Jesus teach about the Old Testament?

24 Define the Greek word *spoudazo* as it relates to studying Scripture.

25 What does Acts 20:32 teach?

26 (T or F) True love gives.

27 (T or F) How we reap depends upon how we sow.

About the Author

Dr. John Hobbs married Mary Etta Palmer in 1973. They have three living sons—Carlton, William, and Austin. They lost their first child through a miscarriage in 1974 and their youngest son Mark in 2015.

John earned the Doctor of Ministry degree with a functional major in "Church Growth" from Harding School of Theology in Memphis, Tennessee in 1990. He earned the Doctor of Ministry degree with a functional major in "Theology" from Trinity Theological Seminary in Newburgh, Indiana in 2004. He also holds five Master degrees and four diplomas from Bible correspondence schools. Including audit, John has over 600 college hours of biblically-related subjects. He has 59 college hours of New Testament Greek.

John started preaching at the age of fourteen. He has been preaching for the Churches of Christ in Texas for fifty-four years. He has helped five churches grow. Lakeview in Grand Prairie grew from 89 to 185 with 53 baptisms over 3 years. Cold Springs in Lancaster grew from 48 to 156 with 88 baptisms over 14 years. Lawn grew from 41 to 86 with 6 baptisms over 2 years. Ninth and Main in San Angelo grew from 65 to 100 with 22 baptisms over 3 years. Cottonwood in Wylie grew from 56 to 114 with 15 baptisms over 2 years. Since 2008 he has been the preacher for the Sachse Church of Christ in Sachse, Texas. He holds gospel meetings and speaks at lectureships.

John has written thirteen religious books. These eight are bound and published: ***The Compelling Power of the Cross***, ***Seeking Spiritual Strength***, ***Building Our Most Holy Faith***, ***Searching for Biblical Truth***, ***The Word Was God***, ***Ask for the Old Paths***, ***Christian Evidences***, and ***Christian Ethics***. These five are loose-leaf: ***The Book of Revelation***, ***The Sermon on the Mount***, ***The Ten Commandments***, ***Advanced Bible Study***, and ***A Greek Exegesis of 1,2,3 John***. All of these books can be purchased from Dr. John Hobbs, 1106 Destiny Court, Wylie, Texas 75098.

John has served as a "tent-maker" preacher most of his life. He retired in 2018 from teaching math for forty-two years in Texas public schools. In 1991, he was selected as an "Outstanding Teacher" by the Grand Prairie Education Association. In 1995, he was selected as an "Outstanding Teacher" by the State Legislature of Texas. In 1996, he was selected as "Secondary Teacher of the Year" by the Grand Prairie Chamber of Commerce. From 1994-1996, John was the Middle School Co-Director of the Texas Math and Science Coaches Association. In 1999, he was hired to evaluate the Dallas Christian Schools entire K-12 math program. In 2001, 2002, and 2003, he was nominated for the "Outstanding Teacher" award at Cooper High School in Abilene. In 2002 and 2004, he was selected to ***"Who's Who Among America's Teachers."*** In 2007, he won the "Professional Service Award" from the Highland Park Independent School District. In 2010, he was a finalist in the Garland Educator of the Year award. In 2010, he was recognized as an "Inspirational Teacher" by the National Leadership Youth Forum. In